An Introduction *to* Linguistics

2009 Edition

Dr. Muhammad Ali Alkhuli

Publisher: DAR ALFALAH	الناشر: دار الفلاح للنشر والتوزيع
P.O. Box 818	ص. ب 818
Swaileh11910	صويلح 11910
Jordan	الأردن
Tel & Fax 009626-5411547	هاتف وفاكس 009626-5411547
E-mail: books@daralfalah.com	
Website: www.daralfalah.com	

بموجب القانون، يُمنع تصوير الكتاب أو أي جزء منه.

2009 Edition

Publisher: DAR ALFALAH P.O.Box 818 Swaileh11910 Jordan Tel & Fax 009626-5411547	الناشر: دار الفلاح للنشر والتوزيع ص.ب 818 صويلح 11910 الأردن هاتف وفاكس 009626-5411547

E-mail: books@daralfalah.com

Website: www.daralfalah.com

رقم الإيداع لدى دائرة المكتبة الوطنية (الاردن)
٢٠٠٦/٨/ ٢٣٨٧

421

Al-Khuli, Muhammad Ali
An Introduction to Linguistics, Muhammad
Ali Alkhuli. 3rd y ed.
Amman: Dar Alfalah, 2006.

(210)P

Deposit No.: 2387/8/2006.
Descriptors: \English Language
\Linguistics\\Education

** تم اعداد بيانات الفهرسة والتصنيف الاولية من قبل دائرة المكتبة الوطنية، عمان، الاردن

رقم الإجازة المتسلسل لدى دائرة المطبوعات والنشر (الأردن)   ٢٠٠٦/٨/٣٠٥١

ISBN	9957 - 401 - 63 - 7	(ردمك)

PREFACE

This book is meant to be an introduction to the field of linguistics, and, therefore, it has come adequately brief. If detailed discussion had been aimed at, a whole book would have been needed to cover what is discussed in each single chapter.

The first chapter deals with the nature of language, its main features, types, functions, generalities, peculiarities, and the various branches of theoretical and applied linguistics. The second chapter deals with phonetics; the third, phonemics; the fourth, morphology; the fifth, syntax; the sixth, semantics; the seventh, the origin of language and language families; the eighth, the social aspect of language; the ninth, writing; the tenth, language acquisition, which falls under the umbrella of psycholinguistics.

At the end of every chapter, the author presents a group of direct questions, the answer to which are easily located in the text, and some indirect questions and exercises which require some research or independent thinking on the student's part.

The author wishes to thank Mr. Waleed Uthman for his help in proofreading the text. He also hopes that this book will be beneficial to university students majoring in linguistics and any readers interested in advancing their knowledge of linguistics.

Dr. Muhammad Ali Alkhuli
Amman, Jordan

CONTENTS

v

CHAPTER 6. SEMANTICS

CHAPTER 1

THE NATURE OF LANGUAGE

Different sources present different definitions of language:

1. Language (L) is a system of communication between two parties.
2. Language is a system for exchange of feelings and ideas among people.
3. It is a means to expressing one's needs, opinions, and knowledge.
4. It is an **arbitrary system** of vocal symbols used to exchange ideas and feelings among the members of a linguistically homogeneous group.

If we examine the first definition, we find that it is so wide that it may cover a variety of systems including animal communicative systems and traffic light systems. The second definition and the third may include the signals of the dumb-deaf.

In contrast, the fourth definition attracts the linguist most; it shows that:

1. L is a **system**. L is a complex system of sub-systems: phonetic, morphological, syntactic, and semantic sub-systems.

2. The L system is **arbitrary**. English, for example, places the subject before the verb, whereas Arabic reverses this order. L functions mainly by convention, and this makes arbitrariness a major feature of L structure.

3. L is basically **sounds**. Although L has a written form and a spoken form, the basic form of L is spoken phonemes, Not visual graphemes.

4. L is **symbols**. The word *chair*, for example, is not a chair; it is merely a symbol referring to what is called as such. L is a symbolized system waiting for **decoding** by the hearer or the reader.

5. L conveys both feelings and ideas. A lot of what we say conveys emotions and social signals; this is what we aim at when we exchange greetings and courtesy phrases.

In this book and other books on linguistics, the fourth definition of L is the most acceptable definition. This definition excludes the dumb-deaf L, signal L, smoke L, drum L, animal L, bee L, ant L, dolphin L, whale L, and other similar languages. Despite the great interest that a researcher may derive from such languages, such L's lie outside the scope of linguistics.

Types of Language

Language is basically oral, i.e., speech. The **oral aspect** of L is emphasized by the following arguments:

1. Historically, man spoke L thousand of years before writing was introduced.

2. Everyone of us spoke his native language for $\pm$ five years before going to school and learning the skill of writing.

3. There are always million of illiterate people everywhere, who can speak their language without being able to write it.

4. Even those who can write do not practice writing daily, and if they do, they only do it for   limited durations. Everyone of us speaks every day, but dose not write every day.

The previous points argue for the dominance of the oral aspect of language over the **graphic aspect**. Of course, there are other types of language in addition to the spoken L:

1. **Written L**. The written form of language only partly represents the   spoken   form. It does not convey pitches, intonation, or accompanying emotions. Anger, melancholy, tenderness, repentance, and the like do not appear in writing as clearly as they do in the spoken language.

2. **Paralanguage**, i.e., body   language. It is body movements that accompany the spoken language such as the movements of hands, eyes, head, shoulders, and fingers.

3. Silent language. It often happens that we talk to ourselves without making sounds. You may call it **inner language**: language without audible sounds. Nobody can hear you, but still you talk to yourself.

Functions of Language

To see how important L is, let us imagine our life without language. Language, in fact, is the center of our life. With language we convey ideas, facts, sciences, and information from age to age, from place to place, from generation to generation, and from people to people. Without language, there would be no teaching and no sciences

With language we write books, novels, dramas, poetry, and prose. Without language, we would not have books, magazines, periodicals, dictionaries, or encyclopedias. With language, we express our feelings. needs, opinions, and attitudes and ask for our rights. With language, we sing, speak, read, write, and count. With no language, there would be no songs, algebra, mathematics, sciences, or literature. Indeed, language is life, and life is language.

Levels of Language

Language manifests itself in several levels in hierarchy: the phonemic level, morphological level, lexical level, and syntactic level.

4

1. Phonemic level. Here we use **phonemes,** the smallest linguistic units, such as /s/, /b/, /k/, and /i/. Language is similar to matter: if we analyze matter, we get molecules, which if further analyzed give atoms, which if further analyzed give electronics, protons, and neutrons. The lowest level in language is the phonemic level.

2. Morphological level. When phonemes get together, they make **morphemes,** i.e., the smallest meaningful units. For example, *book* is a morpheme, and so is *dis-* , *in-* ,*-ion,-ity*, or *-ness*.

3. Lexical level. When morphemes are combined together, they make words, i.e., **lexemes.** The words *continuous, discourage, encouragement,* and *improbability* are made of two morphemes or more each.

4. Syntactic level. When words get together, they form a sentence at the syntactic level.

The phonemic level is discussed by **phonetics** and **phonemics**. The morphological level is discussed by **morphology**. The lexical level is discussed by morphology, syntax, and **semantics.** Finally, the syntactic level is discussed by **syntax.**

Hierarchy of Language

Language is a hierarchical system graded from the smallest units up to the largest ones:

1. Phoneme. The phoneme is the smallest linguistic unit . Nothing in language is smaller than phonemes such as /p/, /s/, /k/, and/t/.

2. Syllable. Phonemes combine together to build up a syllable, e.g., *syn + tax, win + dow, mor + pho + lo + gi + cal, sen + tence.* A syllable may be a morpheme and may be not.

3. Morpheme. Syllables combine to build up a morpheme although some morphemes consist of one syllable only, e.g., *this, second.*

4. Word. Morphemes combine to build up a word although some words consist of one morpheme only, e.g., *geological, philosophical, nationalization, come.*

5. Sentence. Words string together horizontally in a certain order to form a sentence.

6. Paragraph. Sentences combine together in a certain meaningful order to make a unified coherent paragraph.

7. Essay. Paragraphs follow one another in a certain logical order to make an essay.

In all previous levels, lower units concatenate to make higher units in obedience to certain rules within the phonemic, syllabic, morphological, lexical, sentential, Paragraph, and essay systems, respectively. Any violation of these rules will render the output incorrect and unacceptable.

Knowing a Language

When we state that a person knows a language, this knowledge involves knowing these four basic skills:

1. Skill of listening. It is the ability to understand what is heard. Listening is the first skill acquired by the child; he listens before he speaks, reads, or writes.

2. Skill of speech. It is the ability to produce language orally. Developmentally, it follows the skill of listening; the child speaks after he listens.

3. Skill of reading. It is the ability of decoding the written language symbols, i.e., graphemes, and thus comprehending the written message.

4. Skill of writing. It is the ability to express oneself in the graphic form.

The four basic skills may be classified into two types. The first type is the **receptive skills** : the skill of listening, where the ear receives the oral message, and the skill of reading, where the eye receive the graphic message. Such skills are sometimes referred to as the **passive skills**, which in fact are not very much passive. The second type is the **productive** or **expressive skills** : the skill of speech, where we express ourselves orally, and the skill of writing, where we express ourselves graphically. Productive skills are sometimes called **active skills**.

However, people differ in the number of language skills which they master and in the degree of that mastery. There are different categories of people. Some master the **four skills**. Some cannot listen simply because they cannot hear. The dumb, of course, lack the skill of speech. The illiterate cannot read or write. Those who can read vary in their reading ability with respect to speed and comprehension. Those who can write vary as to the degree and quality of their writing ability. Those who can listen vary in speed, effect, and content quality. Those who can listen vary in the speed and degree of their **listening comprehension.**

Dialects

There is no language without dialects. The main reasons for the existence of dialects are the spatially-wide spread of language across countries, the temporally-long extension across centuries, and the great multitude of speakers. A language spoken by millions of people, sometimes hundreds of millions, cannot possibly be produced in one unified manner. It is often spoken across vast geographical areas across lengthy consecutive centuries. The factors of place and time inevitably have their strong influence on language. Further, dialects may manifest themselves in different ways:

1. **Geographical dialects**. Almost every language secretes geographical or regional dialects. English, for example has Canadian English, British English, American English, Australian English, and Indian English, let alone dozens of other dialects all over the world. Another example is Arabic, which has Egyptian Arabic, Syrian Arabic, Iraqi Arabic, Sudanese Arabic, and many other varieties. In fact, within every dialects, there are **sub-dialects** as well. For instance, American English has the eastern, mid, and western sub-dialects.

There are two main principles that govern geographical dialects. The first principle is related to the number of such dialects. The wider a populated area is, the more geographical dialects its language has. The second principle is related to the different degree. The larger the spatial distance between two dialects is, the more different they are.

2. **Social dialects.** Every social group speaks the language in a different way. Language reflects the socio-economic level of the speaker. Educated people speak the language differently from illiterate people ,for example.

3. **Standard dialects.** It is the highest form of language, the language of broadcast news, formal speeches, and university lectures.

4. **Colloquial dialects**. It is language as spoken at home and market. It is the everyday **informal language**, the language which people casually use with their friend. The colloquial dialects is in **complementary distribution** with the standard dialects of the same language. This complementary distribution means that the standard dialect and the colloquial dialect divide areas of usage, and neither of them is used where the other is. There are situations where only the Colloquial dialect may be used and situations where only the standard dialect may be used. If usage rules are violated, linguistic communication may be negatively influenced.

5. **Individual dialects**, i.e., idiolect. Every speaker of a certain language speaks it in a way unique to himself. No two individuals speak a language in exactly the same way. If a language is spoken by 500 million people, it surely has

500 million **idiolects**. That is why we can often identify a person solely through his voice with its unique sound articulations, unique speed, unique degree of resonance and nasality, and many other sound qualities, whish, when mixed together, produce a really unique idiolect.

Generativity of Language

How many sentences do you produce daily , weekly, yearly, and through all the years of you life, in speaking and in writing ? The number exceeds millions and millions of them. Add to this number what millions of people other than you do produce. This makes the number a matter of billions of different sentences produced daily.

If all times and all millions of speaker of a certain language are taken into consideration, the number of produced sentences is **infinite**, as a matter of fact. Despite this infinity in number, a lot of these sentence are new with regard to length, content, vocabulary usage, style, syntax, or figures of speech. This never-ending **novelty** is what marks language generativity. There are always new sentences that are produced somewhere and somehow by someone for the first time.

This endless **generative power** of language is achieved partly by the creative nature of the human mind and partly by the flexible nature of language itself. The phonemes of any language are limited in number, so are its morphemes and lexemes, i.e., words. That is why there are dictionaries that enlist the generally limited number of words of a certain language. In contrast, we do not have, in fact will never have, a dictionary of sentences simply because, and partly so, the sentences of any language are limitless in number and unpredictable in length, vocabulary, content, and structure.

Competence and Performance

Linguistic competence is an epistemological ability enjoyed by the individual speaking any language. This ability originates from two sources: **language innateness** and **language experience**. Man, by his very nature, is created with the innate linguistic ability. However, innateness cannot function by itself if the child is not exposed to adequate linguistic experiences. Innateness alone is not enough and experience alone is not enough. It is the two combined that create linguistic competence.

Linguistic competence is the actual language units stored in the brain in the form of phonemes, syllables, morphemes, words, meanings, phonetic rules, morphological rules, syntactic rules, semantic rules, proverbs, poetry, and information. Competence is made possible through the innate ability planted by God in the human nature, this ability which makes language as such a unique human behavior and not an animal behavior. However, innateness should be supplemented by **linguistic exposure** so as to secure the essential **linguistic input**, which later extends and grows through the creative mental operations of the individual, whose brain cannot but analyze, synthesize, conclude, exclude, generalize, and build rules, systems, and sub-systems.

When linguistic competence is mature enough, **performance** begins to materialize in the form of speech, writing, listening, and reading. While competence is mentally latent, performance, by definition, is explicit. The only way to measure and reveal competence is to channel it into performance.

Generalities of Language

Linguistic talk about approximately 3000 languages all over the world now. Although each language has its own peculiarities, languages definitely have common characteristics usually called **language generalities** or **language universals**. All languages have verbs, nouns, pronouns, adjectives, adverbs of place, adverbs of time, conjunctions, prepositions, sometimes postpositions, and objects. All languages have agents, i.e., doers, and instruments. All languages have phonemes, morphemes, words, and sentences. All languages are hierarchically structured. Such common aspects could be language universals.

Peculiarities of Language

Despite some common qualities among languages, each language has its own characteristic features. **Phonemically,** each language has a certain number of phonemes. Some languages have six vowels; some, three; some, twelve. Each language has its own set of consonants and its own rules of horizontal stringing of phonemes.

Further, each language does or may have its unique phonemes. For example, Arabic has the phonemes /D, H, x, 9/, which do not exist in English. English has the phonenes /č , ŋ , v /, which do not exist in Arabic.

Graphically, some languages have their own special writing systems. The alphabetic graphic symbols of Arabic differ from those of English, which differ from those of Chinese, which differ from those of Japanese.

Morphologically, languages have their own features. Rules of number and gender may differ from one language to another. Languages differ concerning how to singularize, pluralize, dualize, masculinize, and feminize. They differ in the rules of affixing, prefixing, infixing, suffixing, and superfixing. What language X allows may be disallowed by language Y.

Syntactically, languages show more and more uniqueness. Some language begin with verbs only; some, with nouns only; some allow both. In some, the adjective comes before the noun; in some languages, the opposite order is what occurs; in some, both orders have a chance, to mention only very few points.

Semantically, languages do differ; each language has its own perspective concerning life, nature colors, occasions, behavior, and taboos. Culture, philosophy, language, and life intermingle together in avery mysterious receipt resulting in a unique way of thinking and expressing.

Features of Language

There are some universal features that apply to all languages:

1. Language is a human characteristics. It is one of God's blessing bestowed on people, through which they can exchange feelings, emotions, ideas, opinions, and Information. Language is the essential instrument to teaching, learning, sciences, arts, press, broadcasting, and television.

2. Language is basically **oral**, not written. The pronounced-audible form of language has an absolute priority over its written-readable form.

3. Language grows lexically. The **lexicon**, i.e., vocabulary, of a language is in progressive growth in order to cope with new discoveries, new inventions, new meanings, and new experiences. The lexical growth of a language is wholly dependent on the pan-activity of its people and not vice versa. It is the people who advance their language and not the other was around. On the other hand, language rarely grows grammatically; if this ever happens, it does so very slowly.

4. Language is sentential **infinite**. The number of different sentences that may be produced in any language is infinite.

5. Language is a **system**. Language submits to rules at all levels: phonetic rules, syllabic rules, morphological

rules, syntactic rules, and semantic rules. These rules can be observed, studied, and analyzed.

6. Language is usually accompanied by paralanguage, i.e., **body language** or **kinetic language**. During speech, unconsciously the eye express a lot through a variety of movements that send parallel signals matching the spoken message. Face features say a great deal too: the feelings and emotional mood of the speaker are clearly expressed by the face topology. Further, hands, fingers, shoulders, and the head move as well to supplement the spoken language .

7. Language is influenced by the **social context**. What you say and how you do it are strongly affected by the social context: who are you speaking to, your relation with him, and his reactions to what you say. There are different ways and levels of speaking: with your parents, with your friends, with your children, with the mate, and with your boss, just for example.

Linguistics

Linguistics, i.e., the science of language, can be divided into two major branches: theoretical Linguistics and applied linguistics. **Theoretical Linguistics** may be subdivided into several branches, some of which are the following:

1. **Phonetics.** It deals with the production, transmission, and perception of speech sounds.

2. **Phonemics** or phonology. It deals with the functions, distribution, and variations of phonemes.

3. **History of language**. It deals with the origin of language, language families, and language inter-relationships.

4. **Morphology**. It deals with morphemes, i.e., the smallest meaningful units, morphs, allomorphs, rules of horizontal stringing, and, in brief, the internal structure of the word. Morphology and syntax together make grammar.

5. **Syntax**. It deals with the structure of the sentences and sentence order.

6. **Semantics**. It is the science of meaning.

7. **Comparative Linguistics**. It deals with similarities and differences between two languages or more at the phonetic, morphological, syntactic, or semantic level. Sometimes, the term *comparative* covers similarities only, and the term *contrastive* covers differences only.

Applied linguistics, the other branch of linguistics, may have these subdivisions:

1. **Language teaching**. It deals with teaching methodology: how to teach the first language (LI), the second language (L2), and the foreign language (FL).

2. **Language testing**. It deals with how to test the different skills and subskills of language, testing objectives, test construction, test standardization, test analysis, and test interpretations.

3. **Language laboratories**. It deals with types of language labs, their advantages and limitations, and how to use them most efficiently in language teaching.

4. **Psycholinguistics**. It is a combination of linguistics and psychology; it deals with the learner's acquisition of the first language, learning the second language and the foreign language, the mutual effects of L1 and L2,the linguistics brain functions, brain language centers, and language development related to children and adults.

5. **Sociolinguistics**. It is a combination of sociology and linguistics; it deals with language related to different communities, language planning, dialects, language problems of socio-political bearing, bilingualism, and **multilingualism**.

6. **Science of translation**. It deals with translation principles, problems of translation, and machine translation, i.e., computer-aided translation.

7. **Lexicography**. It deals with the science of designing general and special dictionaries.

In fact, there are several perspectives that handle linguistics in different ways:

1. **Descriptive perspective.** Here language, at any level, is dealt with descriptively as it is or as it was, not as it should be. The other contrasting perspective is the **perspective** one, where the emphasis is laid upon language standardization, not language description. Hence, there are

fields such as descriptive grammar and prescriptive grammar.

2. **Historical perspective.** Here language is studied through centuries. How did the grammar or vocabulary, for example, of language X develop through time ? Such a perspective gives birth to fields such as the history of vocabulary, history of grammar, and history of spelling.

3. **Comparative perspective**. Here two languages are compared at any level, which establishes fields such as comparative grammar, comparative phonetics, comparative syntax, comparative morphology, and comparative semantics.

Questions and Exercises
(1)

A. Define the following terms:

1. Paralanguage: _____

_____

2. Silent language: _____

_____

3. Morpheme: _____

_____

4. Phoneme: _____

_____

5. Dialect: _____

_____

6. Geographical dialect: _____

_____

B. What is the specialized term for each of the following?

1. A non-standard dialect: _____
2. The order of words inside the sentences: _____
3. The internal structure of the word: _____
4. A meaningless unit made of phonemes: _____
5. The two receptive skills: listening and _____
6. The two productive skills: listening and _____
7. The individual's dialect: _____
8. Qualities common among languages: _____
9. Qualities related to a specific language: _____
10. Science of meaning: _____
11. The branch of linguistics that deals with Language acquisition: _____

12. Dictionary making: _____
13. A branch of linguistics dealing with the
    function of phonemes: _____

C. Determine whether each of these sentences is true or false. If false, re-write it to make it true.

1. Language is basically writing.

_____

2. Writing does not represent speech completely.

_____

3. The morphological level is higher than the lexical level.

_____

4. the lexical level is higher than the syntactic level.

_____

5. A morpheme may be sometimes made of one syllable.

_____

6. A syllable may sometimes make a morpheme.

_____

7. Performance precedes competence.

_____

D. Which branch belongs to theoretical linguistics and which to applied linguistics?

1. Morphology: _____
2. Phonetics: _____
3. Sociolinguistics: _____
4. Language teaching: _____
5. Syntax: _____
6. Psycholinguistics: _____
7. Semantics: _____

CHAPTER 2

PHONETICS

Phonetics is a science that studies the sounds of language as to production, transmission, and perception. The branch of phonetics that deals with sound production is called **articulatory phonetics**. The branch dealing with the transmission of speech sounds is called acoustic Phonetics or **physical phonetics**. The branch dealing with perception is called **auditory phonetics.**

There are many other branches of phonetics . **Historical phonetics** traces phones back into the past. **Sentence phonetics** discuss what changes happen to sound when used in continuous speech. **General phonetics** deals with language sounds in general, i.e., without references to any special language. **Comparative phonetics** compares two languages or more phonetically. **Descriptive Phonetics** contrasts with perspective phonetics.

Human Speech System

The human speech system consists of these organs, as shown in Figure(1) :

1. **Abdominal muscles**. These muscles push the diaphragm, a membrane between the chest and the abdomen, upwards in order to assist the lungs in the exhalation process, during which speech occurs. The

abdominal muscles then relax downwards to help the lungs expand during inhalation.

2. **Diaphragm**. It is a membrane between the chest and the abdomen. It helps the lungs in the processes of exhalation and inhalation, as explained before.

3. **Lungs**. They are the source of air, the essential cause of speech. From exhaled air, man can, surprisingly, make words, sentence, poetry, and fantastic prose.

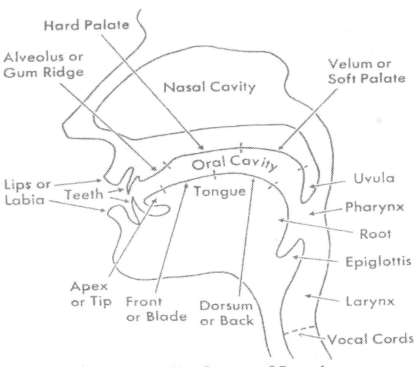

Figure (1): Organs of Speech

4. **Wind pipe**, i.e., trachea. It is the breath passage that lies between the lungs and the larynx.

5. **Larynx**. It lies at the top of the trachea and at the bottom of the pharynx, i.e., throat. It consists of Adam's apple, more visible in men than in women, the two vocal cords, and the glottis, i.e., the opening between the two cords. The larynx is also called the voice box.

6. **Vocal cords.** They are two cords in the middle of the larynx. If they vibrate, the sound becomes voiced, e.g., /b,z,g,d,n/. If they do not, the sound becomes voiceless, e.g.,/p,s,k,t/. You can check voicing by putting your finger tip on your Adam's apple, where you feel vibration if the sound is voiced, or by sensing some humming in the head when you place your palms on your ears. If the sound is voiceless, no vibration or humming is sensed.

7. **Glottis.** It is the opening between the vocal cords. It opens with the voiceless sound, opens and closes repeatedly with the voiced sound, and closes with the glottal sound.

8. **Pharynx**. It is the cavity between the mouth and the larynx. It is one of the **resonance chambers** in the speech system; the other two chambers are the **oral cavity** and the **nasal cavity.** The pharynx functions as a point of articulation for some sounds, e.g., the Arabic /q,H,9/, which are called **pharyngeal sounds**. For the symbols of Arabic phonemes, see Appendix IV.

9. **Tongue**. It is an active articulation organ, i.e., articulator, that plays an essential role in speech. It consists

of five parts: apex, front, middle, back, i.e., dorsum, and root.

10. **Lower lip.** It is an **articulator** that moves to touch the upper lip or upper teeth to produce some sounds, e.g., /b, f/. For the symbols of English phonemes, see Appendix III.

11. **Upper lip**. It is an immovable point of articulation.

12. **Lower teeth**. They are a point of articulation.

13. **Upper teeth**. They are a point of articulation sometimes touched by the apex, i.e., the tongue tip, to produce sounds like the Arabic/t/, or by the lower lip, e.g., /f/.

14. **Alveolus**. It is the internal gum of the upper teeth. It may be touched by the apex to produce sounds like /n/.

15. **Palate**, i.e., the mouth roof. It consists of three parts: the hard palate in the front, velum or soft palate, and uvula at the back

16. **Velum**. It is the back soft palate. It cooperates with the dorsum to produce velar sounds such as /k,g/. It takes part in the process of velarization to produce velarized sounds such as the Arabic /S, D/. If the velum goes up, it closes the nasal passage. If it goes down, it opens the nasal passage as with /n/.

17. **Uvula**. It is a small fleshy organ hanging at the back of the palate. It helps close and open the nasal passage. If touched by the dorsum, i.e., the back of the tongue, it produces a uvular sound, e.g., the Arabic/q/ .

18. **Nose**. It is the last outlet of the breath stream and one of the resonance chambers. If breath passes through the nose only, the sound is **nasal**, e.g., /m,n/. If breath passes through the nose and the mouth, the sound is **nasalized.**

19. **Cavities**. They are four: the lungs, and the pharyngeal, oral, and nasal cavities.

Classification of Speech Organs

Speech organs may be classified into these seven types:

1. **Articulator**. It is an articulation organ that moves during speech to touch or approach another organ, e.g., the tongue.

2. **Point of articulation**. It is an immovable point touched or approached by an articulator, e.g., the upper lip and the velum.

3. **Passage**. It is a passage of the breath stream, e.g., the trachea, the mouth, and the nose.

4. **Resonator.** It is an organ that resonates the sound. There are three of them: the pharyngeal, oral, and nasal cavities.

5. **Source** of stream. It is the lungs.

6. **Vibrator**. It is the two vocal cords.

7. **Auxiliary organ**. It does not directly participate in speech, but it plays a helping role, e.g., the diaphragm and the abdominal muscles.

Description of Speech Sounds

To describe a speech sound, you have to determine these aspects:

1. **Point of articulation.** For example, the point of articulation of /s/ is the alveolus;/θ/, between the teeth;/k/, the velum. For symbols in general, see Appendix II .

2. **Articulator**. For example, the apex is the articulator of /s/; the dorsum, of /k/ .

3. **Manner of articulation**. hat happens to the breath stream? Is it stopped then released, obstructed, passed through the nose only, or passed through one side of the mouth?

4. **Voicing.** Is the sound voiced or voiceless ?

For instance, the description of /f/ is this : voiceless labio-dental fricative. The first word determines voicing. *Labio* determines the articulator. *Dental* determines the point of articulation. *Fricative* refers to the manner of articulation.

Points of Articulation

Language sound are labeled according to their points of articulation (POA). A sound is labial if its POA is the upper lip, e.g., /m/, dental if the POA is the upper teeth, e.g., /f/, and alveolar if the POA is the alveolus, e.g., /s, z/. For abbreviations, see Appendix I .

A sound is interdental if the POA is between the teeth, e.g., /θ, ð/; alveopalatal if the POA is between the alveolus and the hard palate, e.g.,/ ǰ /, velar if the POA is the velum, e.g., /k, g/, and uvular if the POA is the velum. A sound is pharyngeal if the POA is the pharynx like the Arabic /H,9/ and laryngeal if the POA is the larynx.

Manners of Articulation

Concerning how a language sound is articulated, there are the following manners:

1. **Stop** . Here the breath stream is stopped then released, e.g., /b, t, k/ .

2. **Fricative**. Here the breath stream is not stopped, but it is hindered by narrowing the breath passage, e.g.,/s, š, f, v, θ/.

3. **Affricate.** It is a compound sound make of a stop followed by a affricative, e. g., /č, ǰ /, initial in <chair> and <jug>, respectively.

4. **Nasal**. Here the breath stream passes through the nose only, e.g., /m n/, with the closure of the oral passage.

5. **Lateral**. Here the breath stream passes through one side of the mouth, e.g.,/I/. When the stream passes through both sides, the sound is called **bilateral** .

6. **Trill.** If the articulator touches the POA quickly and repeatedly, the sound is a trill, e.g., the Arabic/r/ .

7. **Retroflex**. If the apex curves back, the sound is a retroflex, e.g., the American/r/.

8. **Glide,** i.e., semi-vowel. It is a sound produced like a vowel but distributed like a consonant, e.g., /w,y/.

9. **Vowel**. It has no specific POA and is determined according to the tongue position in the mouth, e.g.,/i, e, u/.

Other Phonetic Features

In addition to voice or voicelessness, the articulator, the point, and manner of articulation, a language sound may have these features:

1. **Musicality.** Consonants are non-musical, but vowels are musical.

2. **Resonance.** Nasals, glides. and vowels are **resonant,** but stops and fricatives are non-resonant.

3. **Aspiration.** If the voiceless stop occurs initially before a primary stress, it is **aspirated**, e.g, *pen*. If it occurs finally, it is optionally aspirated, i.e., pronounced with a puff of breath, e.g., *sit*.

4. **Continuation**. some sounds can be lengthened as long as breath allows, e.g., /s, z, n/. Such sounds are called **continuants**, a term applicable to fricatives, nasals, and vowels. In fact, sounds are either stops or continuants.

5. **Orality**. A sound is oral if the breath stream passes Through the mouth only, e.g., /t, s, I/. **Oral sounds** may be **lateral** if the stream passes through one side of the mouth, e.g., /I/, **bilateral** if through both sides, or **medial** if through the middle of the mouth, e.g.,/s/.

6. **Nasality**. If the breath stream passes thorough the nose only, the sound is called nasal, e.g.,/m, n, ŋ /.

7. **Nasalization**. If the breath stream passes through the mouth and the nose simultaneously, the sound is **nasalized**. Any oral sound can be nasalized if the uvula drops down a little merely to allow the breath stream to pass partly through the nose, e.g., /a/ in *ban*.

8. **Fronting and backing**. Any sound may undergo a certain degree of fronting or backing in submission to the influence of a neighboring sound in continuous speech. For example, /k/ in *can* is fronted, whereas /k/ in *coat* is **backed.** Generally, consonants tend to be **fronted** if they neighbor front vowels and backed if they neighbor back vowels.

9. **Length.** A sound may gain more or less length depending on its phonetic environment. A final sound is usually longer than a non-final sound, e.g., *net, tin*

10. **Velarization**. If the dorsum is raised up towards the velum, the sound becomes velarized. Notice that a **velar** sound is different from a **velarized** sound. Velarity is related to the point of articulation, whereas velarization is an added phonetic feature. The English /k/ is velar, but the Arabic /S/ is velarized.

11. **Rounding**. If lips are rounded during producing a sound, the sound is called **rounded**; if not, **unrounded**. The vowels /u, o, ɔ / are rounded; the vowels /i, e, æ/ are unrounded.

Description of Vowels

Vowels are described differently from how consonants are. To describe a vowel, one has to answer these questions:

1. Is the vowel simple or compound? A **simple vowel** is made of one vowel, e.g., /i, e, u/, whereas a **compound vowel** is made of two short vowels or a vowel followed by a glide, e.g., /aw/ in *now*,/ay/ in *fine*.

2. What is the position of the tongue in the mouth when a vowel is produced ? Vowels have three different positions: **high**, e.g., /i, ɨ, u/, **mid**, e.g.,/e, ə ,o/, and **low**, e.g., / æ, a, ɔ/.

3. Which part of the tongue is obviously tensed upon producing the vowel? There are three types of vowels here: **front** as /I, e, æ /, **central** as / i, ə ,a/, and **back** as /u, o , ɔ/.

4. Are the lips rounded when the vowel is produced? Back vowels are usually **rounded**, e.g.,/ ɔ/. Front and central vowels are unrounded.

Stages of Sound Articulation

When a language sound is articulated, this articulation process passes through four stages. The first stages is the **preparation stage**, when the brain sends orders through the motor nerves to every organ involved in the production of a specific speech sound. The second stage is the **articulation stage,** when the orders are carried out and the sound is actually produced. The third stage is the **relaxation stage,** when every organ starts retreating to its neutral position. The final stage is the **rest stage**, when every speech organ takes its pre-speech position .

Segmental Phonemes

The phonemic system of any language consists of two types of phonemes: segmentals and suprasegmentals. **segmentals** include consonants and vowels, which string together linearly to form morphemes and lexemes, i.e., words. **Suprasegmentals** are phonemes that are produced with and above segmentals. These suprasegmentals include pitches, junctures, and stresses.

Segmentals and suprasegmentals differ from a language to another. This table shows the consonantal phonemes of English.

Table 1: English Consonants

Manner	Voiceless or voicd	Billabial	Labio-dental	Apico-Inter-Dental	Apico-Alveolar	Fronto-Alveopalatal	Dorso-velar	Glottal
Stop	voiceless voiced	P b			t d		k g	
Affricates	voiceless voiced					č ǰ		
Fricatuves	voiceless voiced		f v	Θ ð	s z	š ž		h
Lateral	voiced				l			
Nassals	voiced				n		ŋ	
Semivowels	voiced	w			r	y		

The table shows that English has six stops, two affricates, nine fricatives, one lateral, three nasals, and three semi-vowels. Concerning points of articulation, Englishhas four bilabials, two labiodentals, two interdentals, seven alveolars, five alveopalatals, three velars, and one glottal. Concerning voice, English has nine voiceless consonants and fifteen voiced ones.

Table 1 includes some new symbols./ č / is the first sound in <chair>; / ǰ / in <jug>;/Θ/ in<thin>;/ð/ in <the>; / š / in <shine> ; /ž/ medial in <measure>; /ŋ/ final in< sing>.

Vowels in English are shown in Table 2 , where there are three **front** vowels, three **central** vowels, and three **back** ones. There are also three **high** vowels , three **mid** ones, and three **low** ones. All of them are, of course, voiced.

Table 2: English Vowels

	Front	Central	Back
High	i bit	ɨ buses	u put
Mid	e bet	ə the	o boat
Low	æ bat	a far	ɔ bought

Table   2 shows the nine **simple vowels** of English. There are, however, **compound vowels**, each of which consists of a simple vowel followed by a semi-vowel, i.e., glide. The compound vowel is called a **diphthong**. Diphthongs in English are /iy/ as in <seat>, /ey/ as in <late>, /uw/ as in <pool>, /aw/ as in <how>, /ay/ as in <fine>, /ow/ as in <hole>, / ɔw / as in <hall>, and /oy/ as in <boy>. Notice that each diphthong consists of a simple short vowel followed by a **glide**. In American English, /o/ and / ɔ / are often followed by a glide.

Suprasegmental Phonemes

Suprasegmental, which include stresses, pitches, and junctures, do not appear in normal orthography although they do exist in actual speech, unlike segmentals, which appear in both normal orthography and speech. In this introductory book, suprasegmentals will be dealt with as briefly as possible.

Stresses

English, like many other languages, has four degrees of stress on its words: **primary**/ ´ /, **secondary**/^/, **tertiary** /ˎ /, and **weak** / ˘ /. The stress is taken by the vowel, i.e., the nucleus of the syllable. If a syllable is stressed syllable, e.g., *todáy, engineér, agréement, táble.*

When a word is pronounced in isolation, only one of its syllables receives a primary stress and the other syllables receive other degrees of stress, e.g., *ón, insíde , althíough* However, when words are used in a sentence, many words which receive primary stress in isolation may receive weak stresses within the sentence, e.g., prepositions and conjunctions. This creates two important concepts: **word stress** and **sentence stress.**

Pitches

As for pitches, i.e., tones, there are four of them. First, the **low pitch**, symbolized /1/. It comes at the end of a statement or a *wh*-question. The second is the **normal pitch,** symbolized /2/. It usually comes at the beginning of speech. The third is the **high pitch**, symbolized /3/, which usually comes immediately before the end of statements or at the end of *yes-no* questions. The fourth is the **supra-high pitch,** symbolized /4/, which accompanies interjectional sentences.

Junctures

Junctures are demonstrations of pauses during actual speech. There are five junctures:

1. **Rising juncture**/⬈/. It comes at the end of the *yes-no* Question normally accompanied with a pitch rise, e.g., *Is he here?*

2. **Falling juncture**/ ⬊/. It comes at the end of the Statement or wh-question accompanied with a pitch fall,e.g., *He is here*

3. **Sustained juncture** /⟶/. It comes in the middle of a sentence without a pitch change, often between the subject and the predicate, e.g., *The boy* ⟶*is here.*

4. **Plus juncture** /+/. It often comes between words in the same sentence, e.g., *black/+/ board.*

5. **Negative juncture** /-/. It comes between the phonemes of the same word. It is unnoticeable as a pause, but theoretically one expects some kind of pause between any two consecutive linguistic units including phonemes in the same word.

Questions and Exercises

(2)

1. How do lungs participate in speech production?

_____

_____

2. What are the five parts of the tongue?

a. _____   b. _____   c. _____

d. _____   e. _____

3. Decide whether each organ is an articulator, point of articulation, passage, vibrator, resonator, or source.

tongue _____   nose _____

lungs _____   velum _____

palate _____   upper lip _____

alveolus _____   vocal cords _____

4. Determine whether each phoneme is voiced or voiceless.

/p/ _____   /m/ _____   /h/ _____

/g/ _____   /ǰ/ _____   /z/ _____

/ɵ/ _____   /I/ _____   /r/ _____

5. Each following phoneme is voiceless. Write the voiced counterpart under the line, e.g. $\frac{P}{b}$

p   t   k   č   s   f   ɵ   ŝ

= _____ = _____ = _____ = _____ = _____ = _____ = _____

6. Give the manner of articulation of each phoneme:

/d/ _____   /s/ _____   /b/ _____

/ č/ _____   /v/ _____   /z/ _____

/w/ _____   / ө / _____   /g/ _____

/m/ _____   /I/ _____   /n/ _____

7. Give the point of articulation of each phoneme:

/t/ _____   /I/ _____   /g/ _____

/k/ _____   / ĭ /_____   /f/ _____

/s/ _____   /r / _____   /y/ _____

/h/ _____   /d/ _____   /p/ _____

8. Fill in the blank with the right term:

a. If the vocal cords vibrate, the sound is _____.

b. A stop followed by a fricative makes an _____.

c. The Arabic /r/ is a _____ .

d. The American /r/ is a _____.

e. /I/ is the only _____ in English.

f. A semi-vowel is also called a _____.

9. What are the English phonemes of each following type? Example: bilabial stops /p,b/.

a. semi-vowels

b. nasals

c. glottals

d. affricates

e. voiceless fricatives

f. voiced fricatives

g. voiceless stops

h. voiced stops

i. bilabials   _____

j. labiodentals   _____

k. interdentals   _____

I. alveolars   _____

m. alveopalatals   _____

n. velars   _____

10. Single out the odd vowel in each group, and explain why.

a.   /i, ɨ . u, o/: _____ is odd because it is _____
      and the others are _____ .

b.   /i, e, æ , a/:_____ is odd because it is _____
      and the others are _____ .

c.   /e, ə , o, a/:_____ is odd because it is _____
      and the others are _____ .

d.   /u, o, ɔ , e/:_____ is odd because it is _____
      and the others are _____ .

11. Write these words phonemically:

each	_____	right	_____	pool	_____
look	_____	late	_____	peel	_____
hole	_____	feet	_____	low	_____
caught	_____	height	_____	law	_____
sat	_____	how	_____	toy	_____
let	_____	sign	_____	saw	_____

12. Place the primary stress on the right syllable of each word. Example: fóotball.

isolation	holiday	library
sentence	yearly	university
international	tomorrow	department

CHAPTER 3

PHONEMICS

The phoneme is an abstract sound that has no actual existence in performance. When we actually speak, we produce allophones, not phonemes. The **phoneme** is the smallest indivisible linguistic unit; it has no meaning, but it has a linguistic function : replacing a phoneme with another in a certain word changes meaning, e.g., *tin/ten ,sit/ sat, how/now, sold/ bold.*

The phoneme is defined as a group of phonetically similar sounds in **complementary distribution** or free variation. Look at these words : *ten, stem, bit.* When we say /t/ in /ten/, we produce it with a puff of air; this /t/ is aspirated. /t/ in /stem/ is unaspirated. /t/ in /bit/ is unreleased.

Therefore, we have three varieties of /t/. First, in the initial position, we have the aspirated [tʼ] . Second, in the medial position after /s/, we have the unaspirated [t=]. Third, in the final position, we have the unreleased[t ̄]. Each one of the three varieties is called an **allophone.** Each allophone. Has an occurrence position not allowed for other allophones; this is the meaning of complementary distribution.

Phonemicity Test

How can we prove that a certain sound is phoneme in a certain language? We use the test of phonemicity, i.e., the **substitution test**. Take the word <ha>.. If we put /s/ instead of /h/ ,we get a new word with a different meaning. This proves the phonemicity of both /h/ and /s/. Thus, the sounds /h/ and /s/ contrast Phonemically in English. In other words, the difference between them is a **functional difference** or a significant one. Notice that a sound which is a phoneme in language X may not be so in language Y. For example, /p/ is a phoneme in English, but just an allophone of /b/ in Arabic.

The best phonemicity test is a **minimal pair**, which is two words having the same phonemes except for one position and having different meanings. /bit/and/fit/ contrast initially and prove that /b,f/ are phonemes. /bil/ and /bel/ contrast medially and prove that /i,e/ are phonemes. /kit/ and /kid/ contrast finally and prove that /t,d/ are phonemes.

Types of Phonemes

Phonemes are, as mentioned earlier, either segmental in linear concatenation or suprasegmental superimposed on segmentals. On the other hand, segmentals are either consonants or vowels. Generally, segmentals are more in number than suprasegmentals and consonants are more than vowels, a fact applicable to all languages.

Phonemic Relationships

Phonemes may have two types of Relationships:

1. **Horizontal relationships.** Phonemes string horizontally to form syllables, then morphemes, then words, then phrases, then clauses, and finally sentences.

2. **Vertical relationships.** A phoneme can occupy the place of some other phonemes in certain words. For example, the initial phonemes /s, f, r, b, k/ are in initial vertical contrast in these words: <sat, fat ,rat, bat, cat>.The vertical relationship may be in initial, medial, or final positions, e.g., *fat / sat, sitter / sinner , feed / feel,* respectively.

Functional Load of a phoneme

Some phonemes are more Functional than others in a certain language. This depends on the frequency of their occurrence. Some phonemes are not allowed initially ,e.g., /ŋ/ and /ž /in English. Some phonemes are not allowed finally like /h/ in English. Some are easier to produce than others. some cannot be used in an immediate juxtaposition to some others in obedience to certain **concatenation rules.**

All these restrictions make one phoneme more or less functional than another. In English, for instance,/ž / is not a very active phoneme, whereas /e/ is a very active one. In other words, / ž / has a very low functional load, but /e/ has a very high functional load.

Phoneme and Grapheme

As said before, a **phoneme** is an abstract sound unit actualized as allophones. A phoneme is the smallest unit in speech. In contrast, the **grapheme** is the smallest unit in writing, which basically symbolizes the phoneme graphically. A phoneme is heard, but not seen, whereas a grapheme is seen, but not heard.

As the phonemes is actualized in **allophones**, so is the grapheme, which is actualized in **allographs**. The grapheme <a> is actualized in one of these allographs : a, A, *a, A.* Allographs, like allophones, are in complementary distribution or free variation.

Symbols of linguistic levels

In linguistic, certain symbols are used to mark the different levels of language:

1. Square brackets [ ] to mark allophones and phonetic transcription, e.g.,[Pэ].
2. Slashes /   / to mark phonemes and phonemic transcription, e.g., /p/.
3. Parentheses { } to mark morphemes, e.g., { -ing}.
4. The symbol < > to mark graphemes, e.g., < p >.

Distribution of Phonemes

Phonemes occur in different positions in the word. initially, medially, and finally. They also occur in different environments: between two vowels, i.e., **intervocally**, or between two consonants, i.e., **interconsonantly**. Other possible environments of a certain phoneme are pre-vocal, pre-consonantal, post-vocal, and post-consonantal positions. Such positions and environments may have a variety of phonetic influences such as:

1. / ŋ / does not occur initially in English.
2. / h / does not occur finally in English.
3. If a voiceless stop occurs initially, it is aspirated, e.g., *ten, pan, kin.* If it occurs finally, it is aspirated or unreleased, e.g., *lip, sit, lick,* a case of free variation.
4. If a voiceless phoneme occurs intervocally, it becomes voiced, e.g., /t/ in letter.
5. If a vowel precedes a nasal, it becomes nasalized, e.g., *ban, fin.*
6. If /b/ is final after /m/, it becomes silent, e.g., lamb, *comb, bomb.*
7. The English vowels /i, e, æ, a, u/ do not come at the end of a word or morpheme.

Horizontal Concatenation

All linguistic units string horizontally one after another according to certain rules. This horizontal concatenation applies to phonemes making syllables, to syllables making morphemes, to morphemes making words to words making phrases, to phrases making clauses, and to clauses making sentences.

As for phonemes, some do concatenate obeying free distribution, e.g., /p, t, k/; some others have restricted distributions, e.g., / η , h /. Some phonemes are more frequently used in a certain language than other because they are more needed; compare /i/ to / ž /.Some phonemes are less frequently used owing to their relative difficulty in production. Research has shown that the easier in production a phoneme is, the more frequent in usage it becomes. Some phonemes tend not to neighbor other certain phonemes to Avoid dissonance. In fact, some concatenations are just impossible, e.g., / rηžo / .

Vertical Contrast

All units of the same linguistic level can theoretically Replace one another in a phenomenon called vertical contrast. Phonemes may replace one another in a word; /i, e, æ /may replace /ow/ in <boat>. This vertical-contrast relationship is the only means to selection in the process of language production. Similarly, words may replace one another in a sentence. In fact, the process of language production requires continuous parallel process of **vertical selections**.

Frequency of Phonemes

Not all phonemes are equally frequent in actual usage. A phoneme frequent in LX may be rare in LY. If language samples are statically analyzed, one can come to conclusions concerning the relative frequencies of articulation manners, articulation points, phonemic groups, and individual phonemes.

Statistical analysis may answer such questions. Which is more frequent : vowels or consonants, voiced phonemes or voiceless ones , short vowels or long vowels, stops or fricatives, alveolars or velars ? Remember that we are referring here to frequency in usage, not frequency in the theoretical system. Theoretically, they seem equal in frequency, but in actual usage they are not.

Phonemic Clusters

A clusters is a group of consecutive vowels or consecutive consonants. Languages differ as to their clustering rules. Arabic, for example, allows only two consonant to clusters finally, e.g., /nisr/. English allows a maximum of three consonants to make a consonantal cluster, e.g., /str/ in <street> ; a four-consonant cluster is not allowed except finally, as in <texts> .

Syllables

The syllable is a phonetic unit normally larger than the phoneme and smaller than the morpheme. For example, <dictation> is made of three syllables : dic + ta + tion; <impossibility> has six syllables : im + po + ssi + bi + li + ty.

However, some syllables may consist of one phoneme only, e.g., the Syllables <a> in <aboard>. The syllable consists of one **nucleus** and two **margins**, e.g., pen. The nucleus is essential to the syllable structure: there is no

45

syllables without a nucleus or center. The nucleus is always a vowel. The two margins are optional.

The syllables formula may look like this : $(M_1) + n + (M_2)$, where M_1 is the first margin, n is the nucleus, and M_2 is the second margin; parentheses mark optionality. M_1 or/and M_2 may be zero. The syllable <it> is $\Phi + n + M_2$, Where Φ stands for zero. The syllable <for> is $M_{1+} n_+ M_2$ The syllable <a> is $\Phi + n + \Phi$. The syllable <ta> is $M_1 + n + \Phi$

The margin consists of one consonant or more depending on how many consonants are allowed in a cluster. The word <*street*>, for example, is one syllable structured as cccvcc, where c is a consonant and v is a vowel. The syllable <*stems*> is ccvcc. In fact, English has about twenty different **syllable patterns**, which may be discovered by the student upon a little investigation.

In languages in general, the maximal structure of a syllable is three consonants plus a vowel plus three of four consonants , i.e., cccvccc or cccvcccc. This gives us a total of about twenty probabilities with regard to syllabic formation, *three* of which occur in Arabic and *seventeen* at least in English.

Phonetic Phenomena

When phonemes neighbor one another in actual words, they are influenced by this juxtaposition and show some phonetic phenomena such as:

1. **Voicing**. A voiceless phoneme may become voiced if it neighbors a voiced one. For example, /s/ in <*dogs*> becomes /z/ influenced by /g/.

2. **Devoicing**. A voiced phoneme may become voiceless if it neighbors a voiceless one. For example, /d/ in <*kicked*> become /t/ influenced by /k/.

3. **Bilabialization**. A non- Bilabial phoneme becomes labialized if it neighbors a rounded phoneme, e.g., /s/ in <*suit*> influenced by /uw/.

4. **Lengthening**. Vowels are normally longer than consonants; stressed vowels, longer than unstressed ones; final phones, longer than non-final ones.

5. **Fronting and backing**. A phoneme may be fronted or backed if it neighbors a front or back phoneme respectively. For example, /g/ is backed in <*goat*> and fronted in <*get*> .

6. **Assimilation**. Neighboring sounds tend to be similar. For example, /n/ becomes /m/ in <*improbable, impossible*>; the word <*irregular*> is originally *in + regular*; the word <*illogical*> is originally *in + logical*. Assimilation may be **complete** as in *illogical* or **partial** as in *improbable*. It may be **regressive**: the influencing sound affects one before it, e.g., *impolite*. It may be **progressive**: the influencing sound affects one after it, e.g., *pens*, where /n/ causes /s/ to change into /z/.

7. **Dissimilation**. Sometimes, in order to balance assimilation, adjacent sounds choose to be dissimilar. For

example, in *<circular>*, the final /r/ is originally /I/; here *<circulal>* has become *<circular>* and /I/ has become /r/.

8. Tendency to economy.   Humans tend to economize in effort when they or do other activities. This tendency causes the omission of many sounds during the speech process . Words in continuous speech are pronounced in a way greatly different from how they are pronounced in isolation.   For instance, *<and>* in isolation is /ənd /, but under stress it may become / ænd / and in a hurried speech it may become / ə n / or merely / n /.

Questions and Exercises
(3)

1. **What are the three allophones of /t/ in English and the distribution of each?**
a. [   ] _____
b. [   ] _____
c. [   ] _____

2. **What is the difference between /s/ and <s> ?**
_____
_____

3. **What is the difference between /s/ and {s} ?**
_____
_____

4. **What is the distribution of each of the following in English: initially, medially, or/and finally?**

/ ŋ / _____   / h / _____
/ ž / _____   [p¹] _____
[kᵌ] _____   [t˙] _____
/ b / _____   / ǰ / _____

5. **What are the conditions of each following case?**
a. the aspiration of a stop:
_____
_____

b. the unreleased of a stop:
_____
_____

49

c. the non-aspiration of a stop:

_____

_____

d. voicing a voiceless consonant:

_____

_____

e. nasalizing a vowel:

_____

_____

f. not pronouncing a find /b/:

_____

_____

6. Analyze these words into syllables. Example: modernization = *mo + der + ni + za + tion*

previous _____   kingdom _____

translation _____   minimum _____

photographic_____   psychology_____

7. Describe each syllable using the formula M1 + n+ M$_2$. use ϕ if M1 or M$_2$ is zero. Example: on= ϕ + n+ M$_2$.

fit _____   no _____

moan _____   fine _____

to _____   a _____

mark _____   streets_____

8. Describe the syllable(s) of each word using c for a consonant and v for a vowel. Example: kitten = cv + cvc. Notice what counts here is pronunciation, not spelling.

mine _____   knight _____

50

Christ	_____	doubt	_____
cheque	_____	Eve	_____
eye	_____	ocean	_____
correct	_____	occasion	_____
rinse	_____	headache	_____
inhabitants	_____	companions	_____
angel	_____	distinction	_____

9. Is the assimilation in each following word progressive or regressive?

pens	_____	picked	_____
improbable	_____	dogs	_____
illegal	_____	tipped	_____

10. Is the assimilation in each following word complete or partial?

impossible	_____	illegible	_____
illiberal	_____	irregular	_____
impatient	_____	walked	_____
passed	_____	individuals	_____

11. Explain the reasons for these phonetic cases in these words.

a. <s> in *digs* is pronounced /z/.

_____

b. /n/ in *moon* is longer than /n/ in *paint*.

_____

_____

c./g/ in *good* is bilabialized.

_____

d. /d/ in *jumped* is pronounced /t/.

_____

e. /k/ in *caught* is backed.

_____

f. /a/ in *fan* is nasalized.

_____

g. /n/ has become /m/ in *imperfect*.

_____

h. *regulal* has become *regular*.

_____

12. Say whether each pair is a minimal pair, two homophones, or neither. note that homophones are words pronounced the same way, usually with different meanings and spellings.

bill/bell	_____	pond/bond	_____
cane/gain	_____	bear/bare	_____
cane/came	_____	boot/boat	_____
aloud/allowed	_____	skill/skilled	_____
could/good	_____	ate/eight	_____
leak/league	_____	town/down	_____
ton/done	_____	dam/damn	_____
seal/zeal	_____	lid/led	_____
juice/Jews	_____	shows/shoes	_____

die/dye	_____	hour/our	_____
hair/hare	_____	hole/hall	_____
all/wall	_____	mail/male	_____
face/phase	_____	row/raw	_____
owe/awe	_____	ship/chip	_____
shoes/chose	_____	share/chairs	_____
morning/mourning	_____	one/own	_____
pence/pens	_____	advice/advise	_____
loosing/losing	_____	road/rowed	_____
missed/mist	_____	miss/mess	_____
cheese/she's	_____	chose/whose	_____
about/account	_____	whose/hose	_____

13. Decide if each pair is a minimal pair or not ; Write _YES_ or _NO_. If yes, what are the two phonemes in contrast, and what is the position of contrast: initial, medial, or final?

Pair	Yes No	Contrasting Phonemes	Contrast Position
sight/side	yes	/t,d/	final
hole/whole	_____	_____	_____
sow/saw	_____	_____	_____
see/seas	_____	_____	_____
in/inn	_____	_____	_____
might/right	_____	_____	_____
sent/send	_____	_____	_____
tide/tied	_____	_____	_____
since/sins	_____	_____	_____
grace/graze	_____	_____	_____
tooth/tool	_____	_____	_____
bath/bathe	_____	_____	_____

threat/thread	_____	_____	_____
cell/sell	_____	_____	_____
choke/chalk	_____	_____	_____
flue/flew	_____	_____	_____
coal/call	_____	_____	_____
for/four	_____	_____	_____
France/frank	_____	_____	_____
lit/lets	_____	_____	_____

14. Analyze a sample of Arabic words, and discover the three syllabic patterns of Arabic.

a. _____   b. _____   c. _____

15. Analyze a sample of English words, and discover by yourself the ten syllabic patterns of English, e.g., cv as in *go*.

PATTERN	EXAMPLE
a. _____	_____
b. _____	_____
c. _____	_____
d. _____	_____
e. _____	_____
f. _____	_____
g. _____	_____
h. _____	_____
i. _____	_____
j. _____	_____

CHAPTER 4

MORPHOLOGY

Morphology is the branch of linguistics that deals with morphemes. It is a part of grammar, which includes both morphology and syntax. Morphology deals with the word structure, whereas syntax deals with sentence structure.

Morpheme and Allomorph

The morpheme is the smallest meaningful unit in language. Being so, the morpheme cannot be divided into smaller meaningful units, e.g., *chair, door, boy, book, room, window.*

As the phoneme consists of allophones, the morpheme consists of allomorphs in **complementary distribution** or **free variation**. For example, the **plurality morpheme** in English consists of three allomorphs phonetically conditioned:

1. /iz/ after hissing sounds or sibilants, e.g., *buses, churches, judges, brushes.*
2. /s/ after voiceless sounds, e.g., *books ,bits, jumps.*
3. /z/ after voiced sounds, e.g., *dogs, buds, tubs, pens, doors.*

Look at this series of relationships:

phoneme	morpheme	grapheme	abstract
allophone	allomorph	allograph	actual

Morpheme and Syllable

The two concepts of morpheme and syllable differ in several ways. First, the morpheme must have a meaning, but the **syllable** may have one or may not. For example, <*generous*> is three syllables: *ge + ne+ rous*, noun of which has a meaning. The word <*book*> is one word of one syllable and one morpheme. The word <*books*> is one word of one syllable and two morphemes. Second, the morpheme is basically **a semantic unit**, whereas the syllable is a **phonetic unit**. Third, the morpheme may consist of one syllable or more, e.g., *window*, one morpheme with two syllables.

Morpheme and Word

The morpheme differs from the word in several ways:

1. The morpheme is indivisible into smaller meaningful units, whereas the word, if it consists of more than one morpheme, may be divided into smaller meaningful units, e.g., *improbability = im + probable + ity*.

2. Not every morpheme makes a word, e.g., *im-, -ity*. On the other hand, every word consists of one morpheme or more, e.g, *cat, cats*.

3. The morpheme may be free or bound, e.g., *book, dis-,* respectively, whereas the word, by definition, is always free, e.g., *sit, fine*.

Free and Bound Morphemes

A morpheme that can stand alone and makes a word on its own is a **free morpheme**, e.g., *girl, room, desk, kit, let*. However, some morphemes cannot make words on their own; they help in making words, but do not stand as words by themselves. Such morphemes are called **bound** morphemes, e.g., *dis-, -ness, -er, -est, -ity, en-*.

Affixes

Bound morphemes are normally **affixes** added to a **root** to derive new words in a certain order according to morphological rules. For example, co-operation is *co + operate + ion*, where *co* and *ion* are affixes and *operate* is the root.

Affixes may be subdivided into these types:

1. **Prefix**. It is an affix added before the root, e.g., *enrich, disconnect, impossible, compose*. English has about seventy-five prefixes, the maximum number of which in one word is two, e.g., *reinforce, disintegrate*.

2. **Suffix**. It is an affix added after the root, e.g., *teacher, learning, regularity, greatness*. English allows a maximum of four suffixes in one word, e.g., *globalizations*.

3. **Infix**. It is an affix added inside the word usually to replace other units, e.g., *feet, teeth, geese.*

4. **Superfix**. Stresses that accompany syllables and are superimposed on them are considered as superfixes by some linguists.

5. **Circumfix**. It is an affix, a part of which is added before the root and a part after. English does not have such affixes, but some languages do.

Derivational and Inflation Morphemes

Morphemes which are affixes are either derivational or inflectional. **Derivational morphemes** are used to derive other words from the **root**, and they may cause a change in the part of the speech. These are some examples of derivational morphemes:

1. V+*er* → N, e.g., *worker, teacher, learner, seller, writer.*
2. Adj+ *ly* → Adv, e.g., *quickly, largely, actively, carefully.*
3. N+ *ful* → N , e.g., *spoonful, handful, mouthful.*
4. N+ *ly* → Adj, e.g., *weekly, daily, monthly.*
5. N+*ist* → N, e.g., *psychologist, physicist, botanist, zoologist, geologist.*
6. V+*ion* → N, e.g., *dictation, translation, hesitation, articulation.*
7. *in*+Adj → Adj, e.g., *incredible, inconsumable, incorruptible, indefinite.*

8. N+ *less* → Adj, e.g., *plantless, faultless, careless, waterless.*

9. N+ *ous* → Adj, e.g., *courageous, industrious, mountainous.*

10. N+ *y* → Adj, e.g., *windy, hilly, wavy stormy, sandy, rainy, sunny, moony.*

Derivational morphemes may change the part of the speech and may not, as the ten previous morphological patterns do show.

Derivational morphemes may follow each other in the same word, e.g., *psychologically* (root + *ical* + *ly*), *motherliness* (root + *ly*+ *ness*), *nationalization* (root + *al* + *ize* + *tion*). All the suffixes after the roots in the three previous examples here are derivational ones.

Inflectional morphemes function in a different way. Look at these examples : *learns, learned written, learning, books , John's, larger, largest.* These eight words include the only eight inflectional morphemes which English has, respectively:

1. **Present morpheme**, which is used with the present simple with a third-person singular subject, e.g., *he goes, she comes, it eats.*

2. **Past morpheme**, e.g., *dictated, translated, motivated.*

3. **Past participle morpheme**, which is used to make the perfect tense or the passive voice, e.g., *written, broken, spoken.*

4. **Progressive morpheme**, which is used to make continuous tenses, e.g., *is speaking, was writing, will be cleaning.*

5. **Plural morpheme**, which is added to a singular noun to make it plural, e.g., *chairs, rivers, hills, houses, brushes.*

6. **Possessive morpheme**, e.g., *Ali's, boys'.*

7. **Comparative morpheme**, e.g., *bigger, wider, cleaner.*

8. **Superlative morpheme**, e.g., *biggest, widest, cleanest.*

Notice that the inflectional morpheme, unlike the derivational one, normally closes the word: no other morpheme can come after it. Moreover, inflectional morphemes are always suffix, e.g., *swimmer, **dis**graceful.* Further, inflectional morphemes do not change the root class, whereas derivational ones may do so. Finally, only one inflectional morpheme is used in the word, whereas derivational morphemes may pile up in one word, e.g., *goes, phonological.*

Grammatical Morpheme

Some morphemes, a few in number, do not have meanings of their own, an exception to the rule. However, they do have functions essential to the **grammaticality** of the sentence. For example, the morpheme to in *He used to* *smoke* has no meaning at all, yet it has a grammatical function. Another example is *that in He said that he would not be able to come.*

Continuous and Discontinuous Morphemes

Most morpheme are continuous: the phonemes of a certain morpheme string one after the other without any alien phonemic barrier ,e.g., *- ion – ity, -ness, -ical, en-, in-,dis-, ex-*. However, some morphemes are **discontinuous**: the phonemes of the morpheme are interrupted by the phonemes of another morpheme, a case not existent in English, while it exists in some other languages such as Arabic, e.g., the recipient-noun morpheme as in /**maktu:b**/.

Number of Morphemes

The lowest linguistic unit is the phoneme. Then the units ascend to syllables, morphemes, words, and finally to sentences. While English has about thirty-three segmental phonemes, it has hundreds of syllables, thousands of morphemes, about one million words, billions of actualized sentences, and an infinite number of probable sentences. We notice that the lower the unit is, the smaller its quantitative size is. We may call this phenomenon the **reserve-pyramid phonemnon**, with phonemes at the bottom and sentences at the top.

In languages in general, most morphemes are continuous; a few or none is discontinuous . Most

Morphemes are   roots, and   a   few are affixes. Most morphemes are free, and a few are bound.

Root and Stem

If we omit all the affixes from a word, what remains is the root. This can be formalized as such :

WORLD *MINUS* ALL AFFIXES = ROOT

The roots *of internationalization, reviewing, returnable,* and *re-evaluation* are, respectively , *nation, view, turn,* and *value.*

The concept of **stem**, however, is different from that of the root. The stem is the word to which the affix is added. the formula here may be:

WORLD *MINUS* ALL AFFIXES = STEM

The stems of the same words in the previous paragraph are *internationalize, review, return,* and *re-evaluate.* The stem, thus, may   be a root or a root plus affixes. The root of *mightiness* is *might,* but the stem is *mighty.* The   root of *greatness* is *great,* and so is the stem in this case.

Content and Function Words

Content words are full of meaning, and they form the core of the communicative message of the   sentence. Normally, they   include nouns, pronouns, adjectives, verbs, and adverbs. Function words are not so important to the general meaning of the sentence although they are essential to its grammaticality. They partly include prepositions, conjunctions, and articles. They are sometimes called **grammatical words**, empty words, or structural words owing to their function.

The two types of words differ in several ways. First, content words are much more in number, most words in language lexicon are content words. Second, the sentence may be exclusively formed by content words, but no sentence can be structured by function words only, e.g., *cats love mice*. Third, if the content words of a sentence are omitted, nothing remains of its communicative message. However, if function words are omitted from the sentence, the message suffers only a little, a matter which proves that content words are essential to meaning, whereas function words are essential to grammaticality. Fourth, content words in a language grow in number as time passes on and as the language develops, but function words do not normally increase in number with the passage of time. This means that content words make an open class, whereas function words make a closed class.

Active and Passive Words

The words which an individual knows in a certain language are not equally used by him. Some words are actively used when he speaks or writes. The others are passively used, i.e., understood when heard or read. The first type is called active words and the second is called **passive words**.

This categorization is totally relative : what is active vocabulary to a person may be passive to another. Further, the categorization is flexible. An active word used by a person today may be passive later if it is disused for a long period of time. Similarly, a passive word now may become active later if it is needed more and more in language production activities.

Words keep on moving from the active category to the passive one and vice versa on individual bases. This two-way movement depends on the need for the word, the amount of exposure, use-disuse factors, word difficulty, and the speaker's age and educational level. If the word is urgently needed by a person in speech and writing, repeatedly and adequately heard or read, or often used, it tends to be active, rather than passive.

General and Special Words

Look at these two groups of words:

Group 1: *chair, door, window, man, boy, home, girl, pen, book, school, car, garden.*
Group 2: *stress, nuclear, electromagnetic, nebula, proton, photon, voiceless, affricate, aphasia, semi-vowel, diphthong, light year, input.*

The first group is **general words** used in everyday life by most or al people. The second group consists of **special words**, words not normally used by ordinary people. Such words are used in specialized fields like those of the fields of linguistics, electricity, astronomy, physics, medicine, and computer science.

General words make the entries of general dictionaries. However , special words may not, often do not, appear in **general dictionaries**. They do appear in **specialized dictionaries**, e.g., a dictionary of computer terms, a dictionary of medical terms, and so on. When the lexicon of a language grows in number, it is this special vocabulary that normally grows, not the general vocabulary, which is usually constant in number.

Frequent and Rare Words

Not all words are equally frequent in actual usage in speech or writing. Some words are highly frequent, but some others are rare. Many researchers, in fact, have conducted research on frequency counts of words in written samples to specify the most frequent 10 000, 20 000, or 30 000 words.

Different studies have come to different conclusions because the counted samples were different in scope and quantity: mass-media samples, school-book samples, and other sample types. However, one may except the following conclusions from word counts:

1. General words are more frequent than special words.
2. Function words are more frequent than content words.
3. Active words are more frequent than passive words.
4. Easy words are more frequent than difficult words.

5. Short words are more frequent than long words.

Types of the Word

Words may be classified on three different bases: semantic, morphological, and functional. The **semantic classification** is based on meaning. Such classification gives us the eight traditional parts of speech in English : noun, pronoun, adjective, verb, adverb, interjection, preposition, and conjunction, the first six of which are mainly defined semantically or partly so. For example, the noun gives the name of a person, thing, or action; the verb refers to an action; the adjective gives a quality.

The **morphological classification** of words, however, is based on what suffix a word has taken or may take. A noun is a word that takes the plurality morpheme; a verb, the progressive morpheme, i.e., *-ing*; an adjective, *-er* or *–est*; an adverb, *-ly*. For example, the words *books* , *speak* , *hot*, and *carefully* are a noun, verb, adjective, and adverb, respectively, because they have taken or can take certain suffixes.

The functional or **syntactic classification** is a classification dependent on the word function in a certain sentence. Here, words are **slot fillers** in certain patterns:

1. *The _____ can do it.*
2. *The boys can _____ it.*
3. *He is a very_____ person.*
4. *She did it_____ .*

The slot filler in pattern 1 is a nominal, marked by a determiner before it. The filler in pattern 2 cannot be but a verbal, marked by an auxiliary before it. The filler in pattern3 cannot be but an adjectival, marked by the intensifier *very* before it and a noun after it. The filler in pattern 4 is an adverbial. Such **slots** are sometimes called **tagmemes** in the tagmemic theory , one of the recent grammar theories.

Rules of World Structure

Just as there are rules which control phonemic stringing to build up syllables, so are there rules which govern **morphemic stringing** to build up words. Similarly, there are rules which govern word stringing to build up the sentence. These three rules sets make the phonemic, morphemic, and syntactic systems, respectively.

Here is a list of some morphemic or **morphological** rules applicable within English words:

1. Every affix is used with a certain part of speech and may not be usable with other parts. For example, *-let* is added to root nouns, e.g., leaflet, booklet; -ness, to adjectives, e.g., *smallness, greatness; -en*, to adjectives, e.g., *widen, blacken, whiten.*

2. Every affix has a specified position in relation to the root. Some affixes come only before the root; some, only after it; some, only inside it. These affixes are called prefixes, suffixes, and infixes, respectively.

3. Derivational suffixes precede inflectional ones inside the word structure, e.g., *widens, meetings, psychologists*.

4. Normally, no affix may follow the inflectional suffix, which closes the word, e.g., *harder, softest, walking, goes*.

5. The verb-forming suffix precedes the noun-forming suffix, e.g., *simple + **ify** + cation , pure + **ify** + cation*

6. The adjective-forming suffix precedes the adverb-forming suffix, e.g., *care + **ful** + ly, care + **less** + ly*.

7. The stem-forming affix comes at the end of the stem involved, e.g., *therm + **0** + meter, speed +**0**+ meter, bar + **0** + meter*.

Distribution of the Morpheme

Word-structure rules necessitate certain distribution of different morphemes. Whether the morpheme is free or bound, it has to obey distributive restrictions.

Here are some examples of such restrictions presented by the following ungrammatical sentences:

1.* *They not go*. The negator *not* must follow an auxiliary.
2.* *Boy the is late* .The determiner *the* must precedethe noun.
3.* *He tried do to it*. The infinitive maker *to* must precede the verb.

4.* *She went never to school.* The negator *never* must precede the finite verb.

All language units, including morphemes, are not free in their distribution within the **intra-word structure** and outside the word, i.e., as separate word entities within the sentence. All those units must obey certain rules at all levels.

Morphophonemic Rules

When morphemes are strung together in one word, the new environment may entail some phonemic changes since neighboring sounds do affect each other. Here are some examples:

   1. *in + possible* → *impossible*. Here the alveolar /n/ becomes the **bilabial** /m/ to be similar to /p/ in billability, i.e., the point of articulation.
   2. *dog + s → dogs*. Here the voiceless /s/ becomes /z/ to be similar to /g/ in voicing.
   3. *push + ed → pushed*. Here the voiced /d/ becomes the voiceless /t/ to be similar to / š / in voicelessness.
   4. *circle + al → circular*. Here /al/ becomes /ar/ to be dissimilar to /I/ in the word circle.

In   fact, there are   many examples which   show morphophonemic rules at work, e.g., *in + legal → illegal, in regular → irregular , in + probable → improbable , he + objective case → him, he + genitive → his, they + objective case → them.*

Word Coinage

New words are always added to language lexicon through one of these ways:

1. **Derivation**. The users of a language often feel free to invent new words through analogy with established language patterns. For example, the suffix *-ize* is added to adjectives to derive verbs such as *americanize, arabicize, nationalize, naturalize, internationalize, modernize*, Some words come up into usage for the first time as a result of an analogical process of some kind.

Nouns may be derived from verbs, e.g., *dictation, arrival, worker, from nouns, e.g. , psychologist , historian,* or from adjectives, e.g., *popularity , greatness*. Verbs may be derived from adjectives, e.g., *enrich, widen , simplify, or from nouns, e.g., ionize, atomize*. Adjectives may be derived from nouns, e.g., *mathematical, geographical, natural, windy, beautiful,* or from verbs, e.g., *readable, comprehensible, interesting.*

2. **Invested derivation** or back-formation. Such derivation goes in the opposite, unexpected, direction. For instance, nouns are normally derived from verbs, but it may happen that some verbs are derived from nouns e.g., *edit, hawk, enthuse from editor, hawker, enthusiasm*, respectively. It is derivation by omission, not by addition.

3. **Inflation**. Many words are built through inflectional affixation, where the same part of speech comes, as an

output of the inflation, with a modified meaning . Plural nouns are derived from singular nouns through inflectional suffixes, e.g., *boys, children, oxen, feet*. The present participle and the past participle are derived from the present form of the verb , e.g., *teaching, walking, gone, written*. The past form is derived from the present form through inflectional suffixes or affixes, e.g., *learned, went, spoke*. Comparative and superlative adjectives are derived from positive adjectives through inflection also, e.g. , *greater, greatest*.

4. Compounds. Two words are combined together to make a compound. These compounding process may take a variety of forms:

a. Noun + Noun → Noun, e.g., *football, classroom, rainbow, tablecloth, classmate* .

b. Adjective + Adjective → Adjective, e.g., *icy-cold, red-hot, bittersweet.*

c. Noun + Adjective → Adjective, e.g., *watertight, lifelong, headstrong.*

d. Verb + Noun → Noun, e.g., *pickpocket, daredevil.*

e. Adjective + Noun → Noun , e.g., *blackboard, poorhouse, whiteboard.*

f. Adjective + Verb → Adjective, e.g., *highborn.*

g. Noun + Verb → Verb, e.g., *spoonfeed, brainwash, daydream.*

h. Verb + Verb → Verb, e.g., *sleepwalk.*

5. Acronyms. An acronym is a word derived from the initials of several words, e.g., UNO (*United Nations Organization*), USA (*United States of America*), NATO

(*North Atlantic Treaty Organization*), UNESCO (*United Nations Educational, Scientific, and Cultural Organization*).

6. **Blends**. A blend is the first part of a word combined with the last part of another word, e.g., *smog (smoke + fog)*, *motel (motor + hotel), urinalysis (urine + analysis)*.

7. **Abbreviation** or clipping. A word is coined by abbreviating another word retaining the same meaning, e.g., *telly* from *television, Prof* from *professor, tech* from *technology, math* from *mathematics, ad* from *advertisement, phone* from *telephone, flue* from *influenza, gym* from *gymnasium.*

Questions and Exercises
(4)

1. **What are the three allomorphs of the plurality morpheme in English, and how is each distributed?**

a. /   / _____

b. /   / _____

c. /   / _____

2. **Divide each word into its morphemes. Example: Friendly=friend + ly.**

ordinarily	_____	sparingly	_____
paragraph	_____	communications	_____
rebuilding	_____	degradation	_____
unlicensed	_____	acceptability	_____

3. Decide whether each italicized unit is free or bound.

*mean*ingful	_____	continual*ly*	_____
*up*standing	_____	connota*tion*	_____
breezi*ness*	_____	com*position*	_____
*un*doubtedly	_____	sub*division*	_____

4. Single out the prefix(es), suffix(es), and root of each word down here in this table.

Word	Prefixes	Root	Suffixes
grammatical			
mysterious			
impenetratable			
informality			

Words	Root	Prefixes	Word	Suffixes
accumulation				
atmosphere				
overloading				
authorization				
expression				
impossibility				

5. Decide whether each italicized suffix is derivational or inflectional.

additional _____   unfavor*able* _____

preserv*ing* _____   powerful*ly* _____

poem*s* _____   count*less* _____

appreciat*ion* _____   intelligen*ce* _____

larg*est* _____   work*er* _____

smart*er* _____   imagine*s* _____

order*ed* _____   comparat*ive* _____

6. Write the derivational rule of each word.
Example: logical= logic + al . N + al →Adj.

democratic = _____

chosen = _____

functional = _____

statement = _____

americanize= _____

sensibility = _____

conclusion = _____

observable = _____

rationalization= _____

organized = _____

immediacy = _____

7. What is the morphological class of each word?

bright	_____	Why? _____
carelessly	_____	Why? _____
return	_____	Why? _____
achievement	_____	Why? _____

8. Write down the stem of each word in the first column and the functional class of the word in the second.

racialism	*racial*	nominal
visualize	_____	_____
withdrawal	_____	_____
kingdom	_____	_____
hindrance	_____	_____
fatherly	_____	_____
dictatorship	_____	_____
coverage	_____	_____
plantless	_____	_____
carefulness	_____	_____
bakery	_____	_____
courageous	_____	_____

9. What is the last phoneme in each word?

windows	_____	involved	_____
experienced	_____	actions	_____
organized	_____	mocked	_____
sobbed	_____	asked	_____
peeped	_____	locks	_____
photographed	_____	fights	_____
signed	_____	kicked	_____
locked	_____	pipes	_____

10. What is the derivation formula of each compound? Example: blackboard = Adj + N → N.

thirty-two = _____ ⟶ _____

tablecloth = _____ ⟶ _____

waterproof = _____ ⟶ _____

breakfast = _____ ⟶ _____

pickpocket _____ ⟶ _____

war-plane _____ ⟶ _____

walking stick _____ ⟶ _____

headache _____ ⟶ _____

afternoon _____ ⟶ _____

midnight _____ ⟶ _____

sunset _____ ⟶ _____

underestimate _____ ⟶ _____

brainwash _____ ⟶ _____

CHAPTER 5

SYNTAX

Syntax deals with the sentence structure, i.e., word order within the sentence. Syntax and morphology together make grammar.

Branches of Syntax

Some linguists look at language as a human behavior that should be described as it is through observation first and analysis then. Thus, they are very much similar to the physicist, whose role is strictly limited to observing and describing matter as it actually is without any interference in its behavior or qualities. Such syntax is called **descriptive syntax.**

In contrast, some other linguists insist that their role is not merely to describe syntax as it is, but to describe it as it *should be*. They like to function as guardsmen of language purposing at keeping it ideal, standardized, pure, stable, and resistant to the influences of place and time. Such syntax is called **prescriptive syntax** or standardized syntax.

All languages have had both descriptive grammarians and prescriptive grammarians. Descriptions welcome dialects, language diversity, pronunciation and usage plurality, and language change. They resent specialists' interference to control language behavior. On the other hand, prescriptions consider dialects as deviations from the standard origin. They describe a language as they wish it to be, do not welcome language change, and see that their function is to guard the standards of language correctness.

Like other branches of linguists, syntax may be **historical** if it traces the development of syntax along a certain era. It may **be comparative** if it deals with syntactic comparison of two languages or more . Further, syntax may be general if it deals with languages in general or may be special if it deals with one specific language.

Types of Sentence Classification

There are several ways to sentence classification. First, the classification may be based on the speaker's motive and intention. Does he intend to give information, ask for information , give a command, or make an exclamation ? Such classification is called **psychological classification**. Second, the classification may be based on sentence structure. Is it simple, compound, or complex ? How many verbs are there in the sentence? Does the sentence include other sentences? Such classification is called **structural classification**. Third, the sentence may be classified according to its beginning. This may be called the **initial classification**.

Psychological Classification

According to the psychological classification of sentences, we may have the following types:

1. **Informative sentence, i.e.**, statement. Here the speaker wants to tell someone something, give information, or express his opinions, feelings, or attitudes:

His father left yesterday. (information)
I do care for you. (feelings)
You had better postpone the game. (opinion)
The Arabs must unit themselves. (attitude)

2. **Interrogative sentence.** Here the sentence producer asks about someone ,time, place, instrument, reason, manner, or anything else:

Who did it? (person)
When did he arrive?(time)
Where is he ? (place)
What did you write with ? (instrument)
Why is he late ? (reason)
How did she swim ? (manner)

3. **Exclamatory sentence.** Here the sentence producer express his surprise or admiration, e.g., *What a car this is!*

4. **Imperative sentence**, i.e, command. Here the speaker or the writer offers a request or gives a command depending on the speaker-hearer relationship:

Open the door, please. (request)
Do it now. (command)

Some sentences, however, have a double role. Here are some examples:

A. *Why is the professor late ?* This sentence is basically Interrogative, yet it informs that *the professor is late*.

B. *Will you open the window* ? This sentence is obviously a question, yet it implies a request, not a question.

C. *What a beautiful car you have!* This sentence is an exclamation, yet it states that *the car is beautiful.*

It must be noticed that final punctuation marks are determined by syntax, not by meaning. Sentence (A),for example, has a question mark because syntactically it has a question structure although it informs as well. Sentence (B), although a request, is a question in syntax; notice its subject-verb inversion. Sentence (C), although partly informative, is an exclamatory sentence with a final exclamation mark.

Structural Classification

Structurally, English sentence may be classified as follows:

1. **Simple sentence.** It is a sentence with one subject and one predicate, e.g., *John is a clever boy.*

2. **Compound sentence**. It is a sentence which consists of two simple sentences or more conjoined with a co-ordinating conjunction, e.g., *He studied hard. But he could not pass.*

3. **Complex sentence**. It is a sentence that consists of a main clause and one subordinate clause or more, which may be a noun clause, adjective clause, or adverb clause:

He knows *why they are late*. (noun clause)

This is the driver *whose car stolen* . (adjective clause)
He phoned *when he arrived.* (adverb clause)

Initial Classification

According to the initial word of the sentence, sentences are of two different types:

1. **Verbal sentences** if they start with a verb. Such sentences do not exist in all languages and certainly not in English. Arabic has such verbal sentences, however.

2. **Nominal sentences** if they start with a noun, which is the case with all English sentences in their deep structure, e.g., *The teacher has come early*.

Infinity of Language

How many phonemes are there in English or in Language X ? How many morphemes ? How many words? All these questions are answerable by giving either a specific number or an approximate one. Of course, the number increases as the unit rank increases: for example, 30 phonemes, 100,000 morphemes, and one million words.

How many sentences does English or language Y have ? Such a question is certainly unanswerable. No number is acceptable no matter how high it is. The reason is that the number of sentences in any language is, in fact, infinite. Each one of millions of people produces millions of different sentences in a certain language during his life.

Taking into consideration the fact that the world population is almost totally renewed every century, one may imagine the infinite number of produced sentences. Add the infinite number of written sentences to the inifinte number of spoken ones.

Language has a limited number of phonemes, of syllables, of morphemes, and of words. However, when it comes to sentences, the number is limitless. New sentences are continuously coming up in an endless flow of spoken and written units. The sentences are new not only in their temporal dimension, but also in their syntactic structure, length, meaning, and lexemes.

Sentence Correctness

There are two different concepts related to sentence correctness. The first one is syntactic correctness (SC): the sentence is to be syntactically correct regardless of its content. The second is information trueness (IT): the content is to be real and actual regardless of syntax.

Look at these four sentences:

1. *The capital of France is Paris.*
2. *The capital of France is Rome.*
3. ** The capital of France are Paris.*
4. ** The capital of France are Rome.*

Sentence (1) obviously has both syntactic correctness and information trueness. Sentence (2) is syntactically correct, but informationally false (IF). Sentence (3) is syntactically   wrong (SW), but informationally true. Sentence (4) is both syntactically wrong and informationally false.

Therefore, sentences may be one of these types with regard to correctness and trueness:

1. SC + IT
2. SC + IF
3. SW + IT
4. SW + IF

Syntactic Flexibility

The rules of syntactic correctness do not always require a rigid order of words within the sentence. Different syntactic patterns allow different degrees of order flexibility. In fact, some languages are more flexible than others with respect to intra-sentence order. However, such flexibility is never without limitations.

The noun phrase (NP) in English has its intra-phrase order. The determiner, such as *the , a , my, and this*, must precede the noun head, e.g., *the book*. The adjective usually precedes the noun head , e.g., *the poor man*. The verb phrase (VP) has its internal order as well, e.g., *will have been being written.*   The VP order is this: modal + perfective + progressive + passive + main verb.

The most flexible units inside the sentence are adverbs. For example, the sentence adverbial, e.g., *therefore*, may come initially, medially, or finally:

Therefore, the company was successful.
The company, therefore, was successful.
The company was successful, therefore.

Morphology-Syntax Relationship

Every linguistic level is connected with both the level right below and the level right above. The word level, i.e., lexical level, is no exception: it is an intervening link between the morphological level and the syntactic level. The morphology of a word affects the syntax of the sentence involved . Look at these sentences:

1. *The player is here.*
2. *The players are here.*

The singularity of player in sentence (1) entails the verb *is*. The plurality of players in sentence (2) entails the verb *are*.

Therefore, morpheme do affect syntax. Rules of syntactic correctness require responding to the morphological build-up of words. Any sentence whose syntax fails to respond to its morphology becomes syntactically incorrect.

Horizontal Structure of the Sentence

When we write a   sentence, we produce it on paper horizontally one word after another. When we say it, we produce it orally in **linear succession**. When we read it, we find it actualized horizontally before our eyes. When we hear it, it comes to our brains in temporal succession .

This horizontal actualization of the sentence, both temporally and spatially, ends up with units coming after or before other units. In English, the object comes after the verb; the subject before the verb; the preposition before the noun; the pre-modifier before the modified word; a conjunction between two conjoined words.

The horizontal build-up of the sentence creates horizontal relationships between sentence components. Which affects which? What precedes what? Subject-verb concord is one example of such relationships. Another example is the intra-sentence order. Another is the noun-pronoun agreement.

Horizontal Relationships and Expectations

Horizontal relationships between words inside the sentence entail the positive phenomenon of expectation during the process of reading and listening. When the reader or listener perceives *in order to,* he expects an infinitive. A preposition makes him except a noun. The auxiliary *be* makes him except the past participle or the present participle, e.g., *was written, was writing.*

Such expectations, which facilitate both reading and listening, sometimes lead to expecting not only the word class or sub-class, but the specific word also. Look at these sentences:

1. The student does his _____ before he sleeps.
2. The child goes to _____ every day.
3. The tea was too hot to _____.

Upon hearing or reading sentence (1), you except *homework* or *assignment*. With sentence (2), you except *school* or *nursery*. With sentence (3), you except *drink*. Such expectations, whether wide or narrow, increase the comprehension speed of the hearer or listener and lessen the burden of message decoding.

Vertical Structure of the Sentence

Look at this sentence: *The boy drank milk yesterday.* It has four main slots: subject, verb, object, and time adverb. Taking one slot at a time, we can put thousands of words in the **subject slot** instead of the word boy : *Hani, girl, patient, farmer , child, baby,* etc. So is the case with the **verb** slot; many verbs can occupy this slot : *heated, spilled, bought, sold, boiled, cooled, froze*, etc. The **object slot** can also be occupied by hundreds of potential words. The same applies to the **adverb slot**.

All words which can occupy the same slot are in a vertical relationship, i.e., **contrastive** or interchangeable relationship: each word can replace the others. Such words do make a vertical list.

If we look at each slot separately, i.e., regardless of other slot fillers, the **vertical list** which may fill the slot is, in fact, a very lengthy one. However, once we begin making choices, the vertical list becomes greatly narrowed. For examples, when the subject is *the boy*, the verb list cannot include verbs which cannot be attributed to *the boy* such as *rained* and *evaporated*, except for figurative usage. When the verb choice is made, e.g., *drank,* the object list becomes narrower and narrower because the following object is doubly restricted, i.e., restricted by a human subject and by a verb of *drinking*. The object here cannot be a gas or a *solid*; it must be a liquid drinkable by humans.

Thus, every slot-filler choice within a certain sentence narrows down the list available for choices at the following slots. The earlier the list is, the longer it is. The later, the shorter. Every choice process is restricted by previous process both semantically and grammatically.

Infinity of the Sentence

Some structures may be recursive, i.e., repeatedly mentioned in the sentence. This **recursion** causes the theoretical infinity of the sentence.

Look at this sentence. *The man grows grass, which is is eaten by some animals, which give us meat which is eaten by man, who feeds on both meat and plants, which grow in good soil, which has been granted by God, Who created all beings,* etc.

We can, if we wish, continue expanding this sentence limitlessly. The reason for the potential infinity of this sentence is that it contains a potentially-recursive component, i.e., the adjective clause, a component of which is post-modified by another adjective clause, followed by another adjective clause recursively. Although such a long sentence is not usually welcomed by the hearer owing to its extraordinary length, artificiality, and boredom-causing recursiveness ,it is still a grammatically correct sentence.

Look at this second example of a recursive potentially – infinite sentence. *I think that you think that she knows that Mary knows that Tom believes that Sam sees that, etc.* This sentence may continue infinity, and its infinite structure is caused by embedding a noun clause within a noun clause and doing the **embedding** processes repeatedly.

This recursion causes the **infinity of the sentence**, not in English only but in all languages as well. The sentence length, thus, may range between a few words and, theoretically, millions of words. Such recursion is one factor, among others, which leads to **sentence novelty**: novel sentences are always in the making process. The other factors are wide choices from vertical lists, wide choices for horizontal successions, and wide choices in sentence length. These wide choices at the three areas result in sentence infinity, language infinity, and sentence novelty.

Syntactic Patterns

A pattern is the syntactic design which underlies a sentence. Every sentence has one pattern behind it, but every pattern can show itself through billions of different sentences.

Look at these patterns:

1. Subject (S) + Verb (V) + Object (O)
    Tom + ate + the apple.
2. S + V + O + O
    He + told + me + a story.
3. S + V
    The child + is sleeping.
4. S + V + Adverb of place (Adv)
    John + was + there.
5. S + V + Subject Complement (Cs)
    John + seems + happy.
6. S + V + O + Object Complement (Co)
    They + found + him + guilty.

These six patterns may be called basic patterns or kernel patterns, from which we may derive hundreds of secondary patterns such as :

1. Auxiliary (Aux) + S + V + ...
    Can   + he + do + it?
2. S + Aux + Not + V +...
    He + can + not + do + it.

Which patterns are basic and which ones are secondary is somehow controversial; it depends on how language is analyzed. Further, patterns in general differ from a language to another: what syntax allows in a language may not allow in another.

It must be emphasized that a pattern is different from a sentence in several ways. First, what we actually say is sentences, not patterns. Second, numerically, patterns are limited in every language, whereas sentences are limitless. Third, a pattern may be represented by millions of sentences, whereas a sentence represents one pattern only.

Sentence and Utterance

The sentence, as explained earlier, is an oral or written actualization of a pattern made real in line with syntactic standards of correctness. On the other hand , an utterance is an oral unit preceded and followed by **silence** , markable down here by □ , merely for convenience of reference.

Look at these examples:
1. □ *The boy went to school* □.
2. □ *The boy* □ *went to school* □.
3. □ *The* □ *boy* □ *went* □ *to* □ *school* □.

Sentence (1) makes one utterance bounded by pre-silence and post-silence. Sentence (2) is, in fact, two utterances: the subject is one utterance, and the predicate is the other. Sentence (3) is five utterances: it is spoken very slowly with a pause before and after every word in the sentence. As a matter of fact, a sentence, if short, is said or read as one utterance or two, with an optional pause between the subject and the predicate. However, if the sentence is very long, the speaker inevitably breaks it down into more than two utterances.

Hierarchy of the Sentence

The sentence consists, on the phonemic level, of phonemes combined into syllables. On the higher level, i.e., the morphological level, syllables make morphemes; morphemes make words, i.e., lexemes. On the syntactic level, words make phrases, phrases make clauses, and clauses make sentences.

The minimal linguistic component is the phoneme, which proceeds up in the hierarchy as follows : phoneme, syllable, morpheme, word, phrase, clause, and finale sentence. The phoneme and the syllable belong to the phonemic level of the sentence. The morpheme and the word belong to the morphological level. Phrases, clauses, and sentences belong to the syntactic level. Morphology and syntax together determine the sentence semantics.

The higher the level is, the longer the unit is, and the few in number it becomes. If we begin with one hundred phonemes, for example, those phonemes would make thirty syllables, which would make twenty morphemes, which would make twelve words, which would make four phrases, which would make two clauses, which would make one sentence, here a complex one.

A complex sentence is made of two clauses : the main (or independent) clause and the subordinate (or dependent) clause. The **subordinate clause** functions as a noun, adverb, or adjective:

1. *That he is honest* is clear. (N)
2. He did it *as I told him*. (Adv)
3. The boy *who broke it* is John. (Adj)

Notice that the noun clause cannot be deleted from the sentence because it functions as a basic undeletable

91

component, here, in sentence (1), as a subject. In contrast, adverb clause and adjective clauses, as in sentences (2) and (3), are dateable because they are **optional components** of the sentence : their omission does not threaten the grammaticality of the sentence. Thus, noun clauses are referred to as **embedded clause**.

Meaning of the Sentence

The sentence meaning is composed of **lexical meaning** and grammatical meaning. The lexical meaning is determined by the words of the sentence. However, the **grammatical meaning** consists of these four factors:

1. **Word order**. *John hit Tom* and *Tom hit John* are two sentences with the same words, but in two different orders. Their difference in meaning is only due to a difference in word order. This proves the fact that word order in English affects meaning.

2. **Function words**. Function words such as articles, prepositions, conjunctions, and auxiliaries add to the meaning of the sentence by showing inter-sentential relationships.

3. **Intonation**. The sentence John lost his key may be pronounced as a statement with a /231 ↘/ intonation pattern or as a yes-no question with a /233 ↗/ intonation pattern. The difference in intonation causes a difference in meaning although the words, word order, and function words are the same, which proves that intonation is a part of grammatical meaning.

4. **Suffixes.** Suffixes help the receiver understand the words by giving clues about the word class and word function in the sentence. The famous example, *The vapy coops dasaked the citar molently*, offers a lot of help here. Although the words of this sentence are imaginary ones, the hearer understands that *the coops were vapy, the coops did the dasaking, and the citar was dasaked in a molent manner*. All this information has come through in a molent manner. All this information has come through the suffixes and their clues : the *–y* in vapy, the *–s* in coops, the *–ed* in dasaked, and the *–ly* in molently.

Ambiguity of Meaning

The sentence meaning may be ambiguous for two reasons. First, a word may have two meanings or more and thus causes **lexical ambiguity**. Second, a sentence may be ambiguous, not because its grammatical structure has two possible explanations or analyses. This is called **grammatical ambiguity**.

Look at these grammatically-ambiguous sentences with the two possible implications of each:

1. She made him a cake.
    a. She made a cake for him to eat.
    b. He himself became a cake.

2. Tom saw the woman with a telescope.
    a. He used a telescope to see her.
    b. She was carrying a telescope when he saw her.

3. Flying planes can be fun.
   a. Flying is fun.
   b. Planes which fly are fun.

4. Visiting professors may be useful.
   a. To visit professors is useful.
   b. Professors who visit universities are useful.

5. He bought seven pens and pencils.
   a. The pens and pencils were seven.
   b. He bought seven pens and some pencils.

Syntactic Theories

Linguists in general and grammarians in particular have always worked on how to describe the syntax of language and how to account for it. The oldest grammar theory is the traditional-grammar theory. A later development was the immediate-constituent (IC) theory.

Then the tagmemic theory came into being. Another recent theory was the transformational theory. These four theories will be briefly dealt with in the coming sections. Other theories have been introduced to the field, but these four are more than enough in this introductory book.

Traditional Theory

This theory divides the English parts of speech into eight parts : noun (N), pronoun (Pr), adjective (Adj), preposition(Pre),verb(V),adverb(Adv),conjunction(Con),and interjection (Int). The given order here as suggested by the writer is a purposeful order: a noun may be pronominalized; a pronoun always refers to a noun; an adjective modifies a noun or pronoun; a preposition precedes a noun or a pronoun. Thus, the four parts, i.e.,N, Pr, Adj, and Prep ,may make one group. An adverb modifies a verb; the two can make another group.

The traditional theory has produced important indispensable grammatical concepts such as subject ,object, predicate, subject complement, object complement, and many others . Such terms have a really practical value especially for educational purpose and syntactic analysis.

IC Theory

According to the immediate-constituent (IC) theory, the sentence can be divided into two parts, each of which is divisible into two parts, each of which is divisible into two parts as well. This process of division is to continue repeatedly until the word level is reached. Here are some examples of IC analysis.

1. *This apple has a sweet taste.*

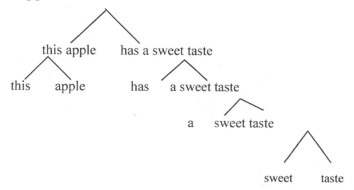

There are several reasons for crimes.

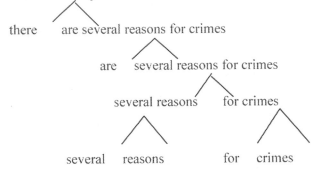

3. This is a modern linguistic theory.

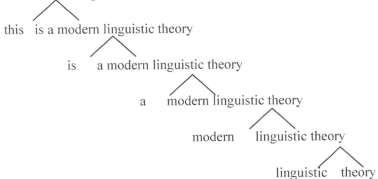

Tagmemic Theory

According to the tagmemic theory, every sentence is seen as an actualization of a pattern made of slots, i.e., **tagmemes**, which are filled by **slot fillers** . Further, the theory differentiates between two types of word classes: morphological classes and functional, i.e., syntactic, classes.

The morphological classification of words depends on The suffix which a word take. If a word can take the plural morpheme, it is a noun. If it can take –*ing*, it is a verb. If it can take –*er* or –*est*, it is an adjective. If it ends with –*ly*, it is an adverb. These **morphological classes** determine the word class with no regard to the usage or function of the word in a sentence.

On the other hand, **syntactic classes** depend on the function of a word in a sentence, i.e., on the slot which the word fills in a pattern. Look at these sequences:

1. He can _____.
2. They went to the _____.
3. He is very _____.
4. He went very_____.

Any word that fills the blank slot in sentence (1) is a verbal. The slot filler in sentence (2) is a nominal. The filler in sentence (3) is an adjectival. The filler in sentence (4) is an adverbial.

Notice that tagmemic theorists use two different sets of terms: *noun, verb, adjectival,* and *adverbial* for morphological classes and *nominal, verbal, adjectival,* and *adverbial* for syntactic classes.

Transformational Theory

The transformational theory, which was initiated in the 1950's by the American linguist Noun Chomsky, holds that each sentence has two structures: a **deep structure** and a **surface structure**. There are **transformational rules,** obligatory or optional, which change the deep structure into a surface one.

Look at these examples:
1. *Tom broke the window.*
2. *The window was broken by Tom.*
3. *It is Tom who broke it.*
4. *What Tom broke was the window.*
5. *The window is what Tom broke.*
6. *It is the window that Tom broke.*
7. *What Tom did is breaking the window.*
8. *Tom did not break it.*
9. *Did Tom break it?*

One can easily see that sentences (2-9) are derived from sentence (1). One can certainly design rules that transform the deep structure into a variety of surface structures with almost the same meaning with different emphases such as sentences (2-7) or with a great change in meaning such as sentences (8-9).

Questions and Exercises

(5)

1. Define these terms:

a. historical grammar _____

_____

b. pattern _____

_____

c. utterance _____

_____

d. complex sentence _____

_____

e. grammatical ambiguity _____

_____

2. Give the psychological, structural, and initial classification of each sentence. Refer back to the chapter to know the sub-types under each classification.

sentence	Psychological Type	Structural Type	Initial Type
1. There are a man at the door			
2. Why didn't you tell us that you couldn't come?			
3. He doesn't know the truth, nor does she.			
4. Go to him now, and apologize for what you said			

	Psychological Type	Structural Type	Initial Type
sentence			
5. How kind you are, and how cruel-hearted he is!			
6. I don't know he will respond to this.			

3. Underline the subordinate clause in each sentence, and specify its function (N, Adj, Adv)..

a. The year when hw was born was 1939. _____

b. I don't know when he was born. _____

c. She was born when he was born. _____

d. I'm sure you can do it. _____

e. I'll call you as son as I finish. _____

f. Although you are bright, you don't study hard enough..

_____

g. That he is honest is quite obvious to me. _____

h. The man whose son was rewarded is very pleased.

_____

4. Evaluate each sentence as to its syntax in the first column and as to its information in thr second column. Use the symbols used in this chapter under sentence correctness: SC, SW, IT, IF.

a. I am five years old. _____ _____

b. The captal of Greece are Athens. _____ _____

c. The poor needs help. _____ _____

d. The Alps is a very high range of mointains.

_____ _____

e. Most of children like playing. _____ _____

5. **According to horizontal intra-sentence relationships, what word do you expect in each blank: N, Pr, Adj, V, Adv, Prep, or Con?**
a. There are _____ reasons _____ this.
b. The two _____ of names do not _____.
c. Ambiguity _____ arise in such _____ structure.
d. _____ doesn't know the answer _____ this question.
e. Make _____ do it now because _____ is the right time.
f. The one who _____ is the one _____ fires.
g. He is _____ than you expect. I know him very _____.

6. What is the underlying pattern of each sentence? Example: I have known him for years = S + V + O + Adv.
a. She made me tea.
b. Birds fly.
c. He loves reading.
d. Are you sure of it?
e. They elected him president.
f. John is here.
g. He is a doctor.
h. She always tells the truth.
i. She seems sad.
j. They found her innocent.

7. What are the two possible meanings of each grammatically ambiguous sentence?
a. She bought plastic cups and glasses.

- _____
- _____

101

b. She called him a taxi.

- _____
- _____

c. She made him a table.

- _____
- _____

8. On external sheets, draw the IC tree of each sentence.

a. This book has five hundred pages.

b. The following anniversary will be on Monday.

c. He worked all those years for very little.

d. It cannot be done that way.

9. Transform these active sentences to passive ones if possible or vice versa. Notice that some sentences cannot be transformed.

a. They went down rapidly.

_____

b. He cut it with a knife.

_____

c. The job will be accomplished soon.

_____

d. They will have finished their assignment by sunset.

_____

e. He saw himself in the mirror.

_____

f. She could move her hand after a long medical treatment.

_____

g. He married her last year.

_____

h. She reads two novels weekly.

_____

10. Transform each sentence to the proper form according to the instructions between brackets, making any other necessary changes.
a. To succeed makes me happy. (*It...*)

_____

b. That the earth is round is a fact. (*It...*)

_____

c. The boy who is standing under the tree is his son. (*Omit who*).

_____

d. I don't know what I should do. (*Omit the second I.*)

_____

e. Because he was late, he missed the lecture. (*Being...*)

_____

CHAPTER 6

SEMANTICS

Semantics Is a branch of theoretical linguistics that deals with the meanings of words and sentences. It is a sophisticated branch of knowledge that touches on many philosophical , psychological , linguistics, and social aspects. It tries to tackle controversial questions such as :

1. Which has the priority of organization: word or meaning?
2. What is the relationship among the thing, the word, and the meaning?
3. How are words and meanings stored and classified in the brain?
4. How words are inter-related meaning-wise?
5. How do words affect thinking?
6. How does culture influence language?

Triangle of Meaning

In semantics, there are three distinct elements:

1. The **thing**. It is the referred-to element, which exists outside the mind and outside language.
2. The **word**. It is the symbol which refers to the thing. The word has either an oral-audible form or a written-readable form. It is a symbol conventionalized by a group of

people to symbolize a thing or quasi-thing.

3. The **meaning**. It is the concept or reference. It is the image, attributes, or abstract entity.

Linguistics, however, have shown some disagreement on the inter-relationship among the semantic trio. There are, for example, words that do not refer to things, such as *honesty, piety, fear, faith, happiness* and other similar words that symbolize abstracts. In this case, only two elements, not three, exist: word and meaning. Another issue is the type of relationship that exists among the trio: Is the world related directly to the thing or indirectly through meaning?

There is a well-known triangle called the **triangle of meaning**, which shows the three elements of meaning: thing, meaning, and word. The question remains this: What is the origination order of these three elements? First of all, we have the thing. Repeated observation abstracts some distinguishing features of the observed thing, which form the meaning. Later, the need for a word to symbolize the meaning arises. Thus, the trio have come into being in this serial order: the thing, then the meaning, and then the word.

This serial order is only tentatively true for a start. However, when the word has already been in existence, the lines of relationship among the trio elements may take different directions:

1. thing → meaning → word. You see a thing, then you remember its meaning, and then you remember its word.

2. meaning → word → thing. You recall a meaning ,then its word, and then the thing.

3. word → meaning →thing. You hear a word, and then you remember its meaning and then its thing.

Semantic Fields

Look at these groups of words:

1. Rose, flower, tulip.

2. Book, periodical, newspaper, booklet, dictionary, reference.

3. Lion, tiger, elephant, wolf, fox, hyena, leopard.

4. Horse, cow, hen, sheep, camel.

5. Hungry, ruler, slept, door, ceiling, man, grew, melted.

Group 1 includes words related to one semantic field, i.e., *flowers.* Group 2 is *printed materials.* Group 3 is *wild animals.* Group 4 is *tame animals.* Group 5 is a miscellany of words that do not belong to one semantic field.

Semantic fields can be subclassified into:

1. **The field of continuous concretes.** It is a semantic field of words that refer to concrete things, the classification of which is disagreed on, such as *colors.*

2. **The field of separate concretes.** It is a semantic field of words that refer to separate concrete entities, such as the semantic field of *plants* or *animals.*

3. **The field of abstract .** it is a field of words referring to abstract concepts such as the semantic field of *virtues,* e.g., *honesty, generosity, truthfulness, courage,* and *loyalty.*

Semantic fields share several qualities. First, the words pertaining to the same field belong to the same morphological or syntactic class. All of them are to be nouns, adjectives, or verbs. Second, the words of the same field are either related to concrete or abstract referents. Third, the number of **common features** among the words of the same field affects the number of member words, i.e., the size of the field. The more the features are, the narrower the field is. For instance, the words under the *bird field* are very much less than the words under the *animal field.* If we add more features to the *bird* such as *immigrating birds,* the number of related words in this field would be less and less.

Recall and Association

When you hear the word *night,* what do you recall? What words are associated with *night* in your memory? Probably, you would recall words such as *sleep, silence, prayer, dreams, sadness, poetry, or snake.* These words differ from person to person and are largely dependent on personal experiences. Such words are in an **associative relationship** with the word *night,* not in a **semantic-field relationship.** In contrast, field relationships are mainly constant, objective, and lexical ones.

Further, associative relationships are temporal and changeable, whereas field relationships are unchangeable. If you associate *brave* with *lion* today, you may change this association tomorrow: you may associate *tiger* or *lioness* with *lion.* Association depends on personal tentative memory, whereas a field relation depends on constant lexical lists.

Another difference is related to the parts of speech. An association list allows in a variety of parts of speech. *Food,* for example, may stimulate associations such as *fruit, soup, hungry, eat,* or *drink,* a list that may contain nouns, adjectives, and verbs. In contrast, a semantic field allows only words homogenous in their part of speech: *food, meat, fruit, vegetables, meal*; here all words are nouns.

Semantic Features

A word may be looked upon as consisting of positive and negative features. The word hen, for instance, is+ animate, + bird, -human, + singular. The word apple is -animate,+ Food, + fruit, + singular. The more the common features between two words are, the more similar their referents are. A *hen,* for example, is more similar to a *duck* than to an *orange* because of more common semantic features.

Of course, some features are inclusive of others by the force of logic, such as:

+ human ⊃ + animate
+ bird ⊃ + animate
+singular ⊃ - plural
+ plural ⊃ - singular
+fruit ⊃ +food 108

Notice that the sign ⊃ means implies or includes.

Intra-field Relationships

Words that belong to the same semantic field show one

Of these relationships, which will be discussed in detail in the coming sections:

1. Synonymy: *brave / courageous, rich / wealthy.*
2. Antonymy: *rich / poor , tall / short , hot / cold.*
3. Inclusion: *animal / lion, fruit / apple.*
4. Exclusion: *Saturday , Sunday , Monday.*
5. Totality: *body / hand , room / door , book / page.*

Synonymy

Synonmy means similarity in meaning of two words or more, each of which is Synonymous with the other. The best criterion for synonmy is the replacement test: if a word can replace another with a little or no change in meaning, the two words are proven to be Synonymous. For example, *he is my teacher = he is my instructor.* The sign = means *is synonymous with .*

In addition, synonmy is mutually inclusive . Every *teacher* is an *instructor* and every *instructor* is a *teacher*, for instance. Thus, *teacher = instructor.* Every rich man is *wealthy* and every *wealthy* man is *rich*. Thus, *wealthy=rich.*

Symbolically, we can express the synonymous relationship as such :

a ⊃ b
b ⊃ a
∴ a=b

rich $\supset$ *wealthy*
wealthy $\supset$ *rich*
$\therefore$ *rich* = *wealthy*

However, some specialists argue that complete synonymy is rare : there is often a little difference in meaning, usage, or both. For example, although we consider *pupil* and *student* as synonyms, the two words do not have the same distribution in usage. We use *pupil* for elementary schools and *student* for secondary schools and universities. Similarly, there are often differences in the shades of meaning between synonymous pairs like *pretty / beautiful , beautiful / handsome, teacher / professor, teach / instruct, and cold/ chilly.*

One can obviously conclude that synonymy could be complete, which is in fact rare, or partial, which is the more common case.

Antonymy

Antonymy, symbolizable as $\Leftrightarrow$, may work in a variety of ways:
1. **Gradable antonyms**. These are antonyms which allow gradability , such as the pairs *big/ small, fast/ slow, old / young, far/ near, hot / cold, happy / sad.* With such words , **gradability** is manifested not only in the two extremes but within each word as well. Notice that such words also called **relative words**: what is fast to me may be *slow* to you and what you consider *fast* now may be

considered *slow* later. Relativity varies with person and time.

As for such gradable antonymous pairs, one of them is **marked** and the other is **unmarked**. For example, *old* covers both *old* and *young*, but *young* covers itself only. When we state or ask, we use *old*, not *young*, e.g., *He is one year old.* Thus, old is unmarked, but young is marked. Similarly, the words *big, fast, far,* and *hot* are unmarked, but *small, slow, near*, and *cold* are marked.

2. **Upgradable antonyms.** Some antonyms are upgradable, e.g., *male / female, bachelor / married, alive / dead, passing / failing.* These words are **mutually exclusive**: if one is A , one cannot be B. it is an *either-or* relationship. Symbolically, it can be expressed this way:

A ⊃ -B

B ⊃ -A

∴ *A* ⇔ B

3. **Relational antonyms.** Look at these pairs: *sell/buy, teach/ learn, speak/ hear, write/ read, give/ take.* If one of the pair takes place, the other must logically take place too. If one *sells*, for instance, another *buys*.

4. **Directional Antonyms**. Such antonyms may be **vertical** e.g., *north/ east, north/ west, east/ south, west/ south.* They may also be **extensible**, e.g., *up/down, right/ left, south/ north, east/ west.*

Generally speaking, antonyms in English are either distinct words or derived ones. The pairs *pass/ fail, east/*

west, brave/ cowardly, and *up /down* are distinct words. However, *possible / impossible, honest / dishonest, regular / irregular, logical/ illogical, able / unable, and fictional/ nonfictional* are different from the first group: the second word in each pair here is derived from the first word by adding a negative prefix such as *in, dis-, un-,* and *non-.*

Inclusion

A word may include another: A ⊃ B, but B does not include A. For example, the first word in each following pair includes the other one, but not the other way round, e.g., *frit/apple, animal/lion, institution/school, plant/grass, flower/rose, furniture/chair.*

If A ⊃ B , every B is A, but not every A is B. the word *animal,* for instance, includes *lion.* Thus, every *lion* is an *animal,* but only some *animals* are *lions.* Symbolically, it may be represented as such:
A ⊃ B
∴. Every B is A, but only some A's are B's.

Exclusion
Exclusion is one of the types of inter-relationships within the same semantic field. It implies a difference in meaning between words inside the same field, but it is unlike differences under antonymy and inclusion. Exclusion, moreover, has several types:

1. **Affinity relationship.** Two words or more may be related to a field on equal footing, e.g., *sheep, cow, horse / animal*. The three words are equally related to the field of animal. The relation among *sheep, cow,* and *horse* is an affinity relation, but the *animal / sheep* relation is one of inclusion.

2. **Rank relationship.** Some words are related in an ordered manner, e.g., academic ranks of university staff: *research assistant, instructor, assistant professor, associate professor,* and *full professor.* Other examples are employment ranks from 1 – 14 or 10 – 1 and military ranks .If one is at Rank X, one cannot be at Rank Y at the same time.

3. **Circular relationship.** Every word here obtains its meaning from its position in a word group which has no specific beginning or end, e.g., *the days of the week, the seasons of the year, and the months of the year.*

Totality

There are , as mentioned before , five types of inter-field relationships: synonmy, antonymy, inclusion, exclusion, and totality. In totality, the relation between words is a whole- part relation, e.g., *book / cover, car / seat, room / wall, body / back, head / face , chest / heart.*

Definition

There are several ways to define a word:

1. **Descriptive definition**. Here, a brief or detailed description is given. For example, *the whale is the largest marine animal, which may be thirty meters long and five meters in diameter*, etc.

2. **Functional definition**. The word is defined by its functional. For example, *a preposition governs the noun or pronoun and puts it in the objective case.*

3. **Demonstrative definition**. The word is defined by pointing to it. *The nightingale is that bird there*, for example.

4. **Rank definition**. A word is defined by showing its position in an ordered series, e.g., *Saturday comes between Friday and Sunday.*

5. **Synonymous definition**. A word is defined by its synonmy. For example, *rich means wealthy.*

6. **Antonymous definition**. A word is defined by the antonym. For example, *rich is the opposite of poor.*

7. **Inclusive definition**. A word is defined by showing the inclusion relation between this word and another. For example, *an apple is a type of fruit.*

Relative Meaning

There are many words in al languages which are relative in meaning , e.g., *far / near, small / large, light /*

heavy, easy / difficult, nuch / little, many / few, tall / short.
The denotation of each word differs from a person to another; what is far to you may be near to him. The meaning also differs from time to time with the same person: what a person labels as easy today may be labeled as *difficult* tomorrow by the same person. Sometimes what is small is larger than what is large: a small elephant is larger than a Large rabbit, for example.

These relative words could be adjectives, e.g., *easy*, verbs, e.g., *shorten* and *lengthen*, nouns, e.g., *shortness* and *length*, or adverbs, e.g., *slowly, quickly*. They usually refer to distance, weight, number, or size. They may be also called **subjective words.**

Literal and Figurative Meanings

Every word has a basic meaning called the literal meaning or the **referential meaning**. It is what the word refers to or signifies. It is the neutral meaning given in a dictionary. The **literal meaning** is actualized when the word is used in accordance with its semantic features. E.g., *He drank water,* where every word means exactly what it literally mans.

In contrast, when we say a *smiling flower* or *the angry waves*, we are not using *smiling* and *angry* literally here. Flowers do not smile and waves do not get angry in the literal sense. These usages break the rules of semantic features, a matter which moves words from the literal – meaning scope to the **figurative-meaning** scope.

In science and informative language, we normally use literal meanings. However, in literature, we tend to use more and more of figurative meanings in response to the nature of literature, which obviously differs from science in both form and objectives. Figurative or **metaphorical meanings** of words beautify the language, give it a special taste, provide it with a special flavor, and make it more flowery, colorful, and emotional.

Affective Meaning

The literal meaning or the **dictionary meaning** of a word is common among all the native speakers of a language, e.g., *pencil, door, car, plan,* or *bird.* Some call it a **denotative meaning**. However, some words may convey an affective or emotional meaning added to its literal meaning, e.g., *home, mother, friend, son, brother,* and *sister.* Such words are rich in their **connotative meanings**, which are conveyed in addition to the denotative or literal meanings.

They affective meaning may be common or private. Words such as *father, home* and *brother* carry affective meanings normally similar and common to all people. Nevertheless, some words have private connotations to some individuals dependent on their personal experiences. For example, the word dog may be associated with horror to a child once bitten by a dog.

Affective meanings may be positive or negative. Words like honesty, *loyalty, tenderness, mercy, brotherhood, peace,*   and *justice* are pleasant words with **positive** connotations. In contrast, words like *dishonesty, disloyalty, cruelty, crime*, and *backbiting* are unpleasant words with negative connotations.

Homophones

Homophones or homonyms are two words or more identical in pronunciation, but different in meaning, spelling, or both. Here are some examples:

1. It is *fine*. He paid the *fine*.
2. *I* saw him with my *eye*.
3. Do you *see* the *sea*?
4. *buy, bye, by*.
5. Have you *read* the *red* book?
6. He *ate eight* apples.
7. It is *right* to know your *right*.
8. The *fly* can *fly*.
9. *Some, sum*.
10. *Hour, our*.

Homographs

Homographs   are two words or more identical in spelling, but different in meaning , pronunciation , or both. Look at these examples:

1. Could you *read* what he has *read*?
2. *use* (V) and *use* (N).
3. *back* (Adv) and *back* (V).

4. *plane* (= airplane) and *plane* (= level).
5. *mine* (= possessive) and a *mine* of coal.
6. *he's* (=he is) and *he's* (=he has).
7. *he'd* (=he had) and *he'd* (= he would).
8. to *lead* and *lead* (= a metal).

Meaning Expansion and Narrowing

As years go on, and new language needs appear, the native speakers of the language may expand the meaning of a word, add new meanings to it, narrow down a certain meaning, or cancel one of its meanings or more.

Language, through centuries, is in a continues process of regeneration: in the process of making. Meanings are added, canceled, expanded, or narrowed. Not only that, but also some new words are added through borrowing or coinage, and some others are gradually disused until they become archaic: no more used although they only exist in language dictionaries as recordings of the past.

Analytical and Synthetic Meanings

Look at these sentences:
1. A bachelor is an unmarried man.
2. A family consists of husband, wife, and their children.
3. A teacher teaches his students at school or university.
4. Hani is a hard-working accountant.

5. Wisam is an honest manager.
6. Muneer is an able business man.
7. Majdi is a skilled engineer.

Examine the first three sentences. Each one of them is true by difintion. It is internally true because it does not need an external evidence of validity. Just analyze the sentence linguistically and semantically, and you find it true on internal bases. Such sentences are called **analytical sentences** wth analytical meanings.

If you examine the last four sentences, each one of them may be true or false. We need an external evidence to verify or falsify each. The evidence here is not internal or linguistic; it is external and data-dependent. Such sentences are called **synthetic sentences** with synthetic meanings.

Lexical and Grammatical Meanings

The meaning of a sentence is determined by two sources: words, which give it the **lexical meaning,** and grammatical structure, which gives it the **grammatical meaning.** The sentence John killed the lion is different in meaning from John rode the lion because of the vertical contrast of killed/ rode, which proves the lexical component of meaning.

The grammatical meaning, however, consists of four elements: syntax, i.e., word order inside the sentence, function words, which mark word classes, suffixes, which mark word classes as well , and **intonation contours,** which mark the sentence type.

119

More details about the grammatical meaning have been given in Chapter 5, in the section about the *meaning of the sentence.*

Meaning and Context

Many words, in all languages, are **polysemous**, i.e., with multiple meanings. If you open the dictionary and look into some of its entries, you rarely see a word with one single meaning. Most words have more than one meaning. In fact, most words have not only several meanings but several functions as well. For example, the word *round* can be a verb, preposition, adjective, adverb, and noun:

a. They *rounded* the city. (V)
b. They sat *round* the table. (Pre)
c. They sat at the *round* table. (Adj)
d. He walked *round* and round. (Adv)
e. He fell down after the fifth *round*. (N)

Other examples are:
- *chair* (N), *chair* (V)
- *export* (N), *export* (V)
- *match* (N), *match* (V)
- *master* (N), *master* (V), *master* (Adj)
- *reach* (N), *reach* (V)
- *decline* (N), *decline* (V)

The context plays a major role in determining which meaning is intended.

Meaning and External Factors

The meaning of a written sentence in a written context depends solely on both its lexical and grammatical components. In contrast, a spoken sentence in a **conversational context** depends on several external factors in addition to its lexemes and grammar:

1. **Body language**. When one speakers, he may, and he usually does, move his hands, eyes, head, arms, and eye – brows. These movements normally reinforce the content of his sentence, but they may sometimes contradict it.

2. **Facial features**. The face of the speaker shows his real feelings such as pleasure, regret, pity, sorrow, eagerness, reproach, anger, sympathy, or weakness. These feelings are manifested in the eyes, which are the mirror of the psyche, and are expressed by the shape which the lips may take and by the degree of tension which facial muscles may show.

3. **Tone**. Another factor that effects meaning is the speaker's tone during speech. Emotions are mixed with speech in a very special manner, and the resulting mixture betrays the speaker's feelings.

4. **Converser's roles**. The relationship between the two conversers influences the meanings of what they say. Some examples are teacher-student, father-son, husband-wife, mother-daughter, employer-employee, and friend-friend relationships. Sentential meanings are partly affected by the speaker-hearer relationship.

5. **Preconversational relationship**. The meaning of a sentence is also somehow affected by the interpersonal Relation prior to conversation. Is it a relation of friendship, competition, envy, enmity, tension, harmony, or what?

6. **Physical environment**. The physical surroundings of conversation may affect meanings. The speakers often use **deictic expressions**, i.e, expressions dependent on the external environment such as *here, there, this, that, tomorrow, today, you, I, we*, and the like.

Questions and Exercises

(6)

1. Add five words to each group, belonging to the same semantic field.

a. gold, iron, tin, _____

b. son, uncle, parent, _____

c. plough, grow, irrigate, _____

d. table, chair, bed, _____

e. pen, pencil, ruler, _____

2. What is the semantic field of each group in the previous exercise? Example: *lion, tiger, fox: wild animals.*

a. _____   b. _____

c. _____   d. _____

e. _____

3. What word do you associate with each following word? Different students may give different answers.

examination	_____	night	_____
fruits	_____	life	_____
university	_____	study	_____
heart	_____	teach	_____
pray	_____	fast	_____
marriage	_____	hungry	_____

4. Give at least three semantic features for each word. Use ± signs before each feature.

lion: _____

thirsty: _____

student: _____

hear: _____

lady: _____

flower: _____

5. Give a synonym of each following word:

debate	_____	instruct	_____
courageous	_____	ideal	_____
answer	_____	test	_____
holiday	_____	ask	_____
think	_____	quick	_____
convention	_____	efficient	_____
retarded	_____	intelligent	_____

6. Give an antonym of each following word:

long	_____	far	_____
young	_____	thin	_____
deep	_____	teach	_____
consistent	_____	crowded	_____
enslave	_____	dependent	_____
hot	_____	high	_____
careful	_____	single	_____
asleep	_____	possible	_____

7. What is the type of the semantic relationship of each pair: synonymy, antonymy, inclusion, exclusion, or totally?

love /affection	_____	truthteller/liar	_____
ask/answer	_____	north/east	_____
active/lazy	_____	fruit/orange	_____
February/March	_____	door/handle	_____

8. Underline the words that have relative meanings: far, city, heavy, beautiful, book , easy, frozen, few, difficult, large, smooth, gentle.

9. Use each word literally first and then figuratively:

garden:　　a. _____
　　　　　　b. _____
mirror:　　a. _____
　　　　　　b. _____
book:　　　a. _____
　　　　　　b. _____
smile:　　　a. _____
　　　　　　b. _____
earthquake: a. _____
　　　　　　b. _____
icy:　　　　a. _____
　　　　　　b. _____
rose:　　　a. _____
　　　　　　b. _____

10. Add a suitable prefix to form an antonym:

pleasant _____ probable _____
ability _____ able _____
calculate _____ honest _____
behavior _____ polite _____
legal _____ communist _____
understand _____ continue _____
encourage _____ comprehend _____
literate _____ regular _____
integrated _____ efficient _____

11. Decide whether each pair is two homophones, two homographs, both, or neither.

son/sun	_____	where/wear	_____
sign/sine	_____	be/bee	_____
sit/set	_____	site/sight	_____
write/right	_____	no/know	_____
new/knew	_____	piece/peace	_____
now/how	_____	sell/tell	_____
night/knight	_____	two/too	_____
threw/through	_____	tie/die	_____

12. Is each following sentence synthetic or analytic?

a. The earth is spherical.   _____

b. A parent is a father or a mother.   _____

c. John is 24 years old.   _____

d. A university is a group of specialized collages.

_____

13. What kind of antonyms is each pair: gradable, ungradable, relational, or directional?

deep/shallow	_____	rich/poor	_____
send/receive	_____	masculine/feminine	_____
fast/slow	_____	singular/plural	_____
forward/backward	_____	sell/purchase	_____

14. What kind of exclusion does each group represent: affinity, rank, or circular relationship?

Sunday, Monday, Tuesday   _____

soldier, sergeant, officer   _____

orange, apple, banana   _____

15. Underline any deictic words in these sentences:
a. Put it here, not there, please.
b. This question is rather difficult for you.
c. Tomorrow I'll be free. We can meet anywhere if you like.
d. Go to the left, and then to the right. There you will find it, I'm sure.

CHAPTER 7

LANGUAGE AND
TIME

Time is the fourth dimension of things, as always said. Everything exist in both place and time. Time works and influences all people and whatever related to humans including language. The branch of linguistic that deals with the influence of time on language   is called **historical linguistic .**

Origin of Language

There are several persistent questions related to language origin. When did the human language originate? How? Where? Was it one language to begin with or were there different languages ? Different theories have given different answers to those questions.

1. **Theory of divine inspiration .** According to this theory, language was an inspiration from God to Adam, the father of all humans. God taught him a language to communicate with his mate, Evs, and their future   children. With the passage of countries and the spread of people all over the world, this language diversified into dialects, which in turn became distinct languages. This   process of diversification was so repetitive and continuous along ages that thousands of languages came being.

2. **Theory of improvised innovation**. According to this theory, man haphazardly innovated words in response to daily needs. People in a certain community accepted and adopted such words for certain meanings. Eventually ,those attempts developed into a language.

3. **Theory of mimicry**. According to this theory, man began his first language attempts by imitating sounds which he heard around, sounds made by wind, water, thing ,nature, and animals. Later , such imitations developed into a sophisticated language system.

4. **Theory of innate readiness**. God created man with a natural innate ability to innovate the tools of linguistic intercourse and the ability to express his ideas, feelings, and emotions both orally and linguistically.

These four theories present four different answers to the same question. However, it might be that these theories are complementary to one another, rather than contradictory . It might be that some elements of the human language are obtained through divine inspiration; some, through innateness. In this introductory book, there is no need to go into future details about this controversial issue; this much is adequate.

Classification of Languages

Languages may be classified **geographically** , i.e., according to language distribution in the six continents.

Second, the classification may be **grammatical**, depending on the morphological and synatic characteristics of languages. Finally, the classification may be **genetic**, depending on the affinity relationship of languages, their descendants, and branches.

Geographical Classification

According to geographical classification, languages may be classified as follows:

1. Asian languages such as Korean, Japanese, Urdu, Arabic, Persian, Turkish, and Vietnamese

2. African languages such as Arabic, Swahili, and Nigerian.

3. European languages such as Greek, Italian, Spanish, French, German, and English.

4. American languages such as English, French, Spanish, Portuguese, and the languages of Red Indians.

5. Australian languages such as English and the languages of Australian native. Some languages, in this classification, may appear in more than one continent.

Grammatical Classification

According to grammatical classification, languages may be classified as follows:

1. **Inflectional languages** or analytical languages. Examples are Arabic, Greek, Latin, Persian, and Hindi . In such languages, the meaning of the word changes with the change of its morphological internal build-up, e.g., the Arabic / *Katab, Kutib, maktab , maktabat/*. Another characteristic of such languages is case inflections at noun endings to mark noun relations inside the sentence. A well-known example of inflectional languages is Arabic, e.g., /*kita: bun ,kita: ban ,kita :bin/* .

2. **Agglutinating languages.** Such languages depend on prefixes and suffixes to change word meaning and to modify syntactic relations. Examples of such languages are English, Japanese, Turkish, and Mongolian.

3. **Isolating languages** or non-inflectional languages. Words here have consonant forms; every word has its own consonant morphological structure and consonant meaning. Words of these languages do not accept affixes: prefixes, infixes, and suffixes. Inter-word relationships inside the sentence are determined by both syntactic order and contextual clues. Example of such languages are Chinese and Tibetan.

Some linguists hold that grammatical classification cannot be accurate because most languages show a variety of characteristics. Arabic, for example, is partly inflectional because we can derive dozens of words from one single root and because nouns are marked by case endings. Arabic is partly an agglutinating languages as well because it allows affixation. Arabic is also partly an isolating language because it has a lot of non-inflected words, e.g., particles.

Further, languages may be classified syntactically, rather than morphologically. There are six syntactic L types: SVO like English and French, VSO like Arabic and Irish, SOV like Turkish and Japanese, OVS, OSV, and VOS. Some languages allow more than one order; Arabic, for example, allows both VSO and SVO.

Genetic Classification

According to genetic classification, languages may be classified as follows:

1. **Indo-European family**. This family includes Indian languages, Iranian languages (such as Persian and Kurdish), American languages, Greek languages (such as Old Greek and modern Greek), Albanian, Italic languages (such as Latin, Modern Italian, French, Spanish, and Portuguese), Celtic languages (such as Irish and Welsh), Germanic languages (such as English, German, Swedish, Danish, Norwegian, and Icelandic), and Slavo-Baltic languages, e.g., Litwanian, Russia, Ukranian, Bulgarian, and Croatian.

2. **Hamitic-Semitic family**. This family includes some extinct languages such as Accadian, Syriac, Phoenician, and Aramaic. Other Semitic languages are Arabic and Hebrew. The Hamitic branch includes languages such as Coptic and Barbarian.

3. **Finno-Ugric family.** This group includes Finnish,

Estonian, and Hungarian, all of which are European languages.

4. **Sino-Tibetan family.** This group includes Chinese, Tibetan, Burmese, Nepalese, and Thai, all of which are Asian languages.

5. **Niger-Congo family.** This African family includes the languages of Sierra Leone, Senegal, Liberia, Ghana, and some other countries. It also includes the Bantu languages such as Swahili, Kikuyu, and Zulu.

6. **Malayo-Polynesian family.** The Malayan group covers languages spoken in Malacca, Madagascar, the East Indies, Formosa, Sumatra, and the Philippines. It includes languages like Malay, Tagalog, and Javanese. The Polynesian group covers most of the languages of the Pacific islands, such as Fiji, Samoan, and Hawaiian.

7. **American-Indian family.** It includes languages of Red Indians in North America and south America.

This seven-branch classification, mentioned above, does not cover all languages. However, it does cover most of the main ones in the world.

When dealing with genetic classification, one may classify languages into these types:

1. **Parent language.** It is a language from which other languages have descended. For example, Sacian is the

parent language of Persian and Pushtu. Latin is the parent language of French and Italian. Hindustani is the parent language of Hindi and Urdu.

2. **Daughter language** or descendent language. It is a language descending from another. French, for instance, is the daughter language of Latin; Swedish, of Germanic; Russian, of Slavic.

3. **Sister language.** It is a language in common affinity with another: the two have the same parent language. Danish and Norwegian are sister languages descending from Germanic. Spanish and Portuguese are Sister languages coming from Latin. Polish and Ukranian are sisters, and their parent is Slavic.

Genetic relations among languages are most probably the outcome of time influence. It is highly probable , for example, that all Indo-European languages were one single language thousands of years ago. Along the passage of centuries, this one language branched into different regional dialects, the differences among which intensified as centuries went on until each dialect became a distinct language. Language is, certainly, strongly affected by time with its demographical, geographical, social, commercial, military, and political factors. The consequence is a growing differentiation in the phonetic, morphological, syntactic, lexical, and semantic components of language. Thus, dialects once pertaining to one language have become separate distinct languages.

Phonetic Change

Along centuries, a language may undergo some phonetic changes although at a very slow pace. New phonemes may come into existence; once existing phonemes may disappear and be replaced by others. A phoneme under certain phonetic conditions may be modified into another.

Phonetic changes may occur due to commercial, military, or cultural contacts of two languages over a long period of time . Another reason for phonetic changes is the natural tendency of language towards easiness. A phoneme may replace another simply because it is easier to produce, and economy in effect is thus achieved.

Phonetic change across time may be reflected by diachronic changes of the language itself. Right now, we do not have any sonic recordings of languages spoken centuries ago. However, future linguists will find such sonic recordings available at hand when they want to trace phonetic changes back to previous centuries.

Grammatical Change

A language may undergo morphological changes. Old English, for example, used case endings abundantly as Latin, old Greek, and Sanskrit did. Gradually and very slowly, such endings began to disappear and the process went on with Middle English too; now Modern English rarely uses case endings except with very few words such as *he/him* and *they/them.*

Morphological changes often result in syntactic restrictions. A language that employs case endings allows a greater degree of mobility of word order within the sentence than a language that does not use such endings. The reason is that case endings mark noun functions as word order does. If case endings are used, as in Arabic, more mobility in word positions is allowed. In contrast, if case endings are not used, as in Modern English, words tend to have fixed positions inside the sentence. Thus, morphological changes through time may lead to syntactic changes.

Lexical Change

Not only may a language change phonetically, morphologically, and syntactically, but it may change lexically as well. Whereas the first three types of change are probable, the lexical change or growth is, in fact, inevitable; no language can escape this change. Further, non-lexical change is very slow: it takes a language hundreds or thousands of years to materialize a phonetic or syntactic change. In contrast, a lexical change can occur very much faster: a language may add words every week, every month, and every year.

Lexical Change May take one of these forms:

1. **New words.** Continuous discoveries and inventions create the need for new technical words. Progress in all areas of Knowledge, moreover, results in new concepts and, consequently, new words, an unavoidable phenomenon common to all languages.

2. **Deserted words**. Lexical change sometimes pushes backward and downward some vocabulary, which becomes no more need. Synonyms compete, and one of them wins and becomes more usable, retracing other rivals only to dictionary entries.

3. **Borrowed words**. People always borrow things from one another. Once a thing is borrowed, in fact usually bought, its name is also borrowed with it. All languages borrow from other languages : Arabic did and does, and English did and does. For example, English has borrowed from Arabic a lot of words such as *cotton, coffee ,alcohol, mirror, algebra, arsenal, admiral,* and *balsam.* Arabic, on the other hand, has borrowed from English a lot of words as well, such as *cinema, video, telephone, sandwich ,fax, telex,* and many others.

Semantic Change

Words sometimes remain to be used, but with some change in their meaning:

1. **Meaning expansion**. More meanings may be added to a certain word in response to growth in human experience. Because meanings outnumber words, the speakers of a language assign multiple meanings to each word, a process which does not cease. It is a process which adds new meanings to old words.

2. **Meaning narrowing.** In some cases, word may get rid of its old wide meaning in order to indicate a narrower

one: the cover of the word becomes actually smaller.

3. **Terminological meaning**. A word may have a different meaning when used in a certain discipline.

Questions and Exercises

(7)

1. What is the geographical classification of each following language: Asian, Australian, European, American, or African?

Arabic	_____	English	_____
Turkish	_____	Swahili	_____
German	_____	Welsh	_____
Irish	_____	Pushtu	_____
Persian	_____	Greek	_____
Albanian	_____	Finnish	_____
Thai	_____	Nepalese	_____
Zulu	_____	Vietnamese	_____

2. What is the grammatical classification of each language: inflectional, agglutinating, or isolating?

Turkish	_____	Arabic	_____
Japanese	_____	English	_____
Chinese	_____	Greek	_____

3. Give two languages as examples of each following family or sub-family (branch):

Iranian languages	_____	and	_____
Greek languages:	_____	and	_____
Italic languages:	_____	and	_____
Celtic languages:	_____	and	_____
Germanic languages:	_____	and	_____

4. Give the family and then the branch of each language.

Language	Family	Branch
Persian	*Indo-European*	*Iranian*
Modern Greek		
Latin		
French		
Irish		
German		
Russian		
Arabic		
English		
Coptic		

5. Give the parent language of each following language:

Spanish _____ Welsh _____

English _____ Ukrainian _____

Persian _____ Urdu _____

Russian _____ Swedish _____

6. Give one sister language of each:

Portuguese _____ Polish _____

Kurdish _____ French _____

Irish _____ English _____

Bulgarian _____ Arabic _____

7. Decide whether each following language is alive, extinct, or half-alive, i.e, of limited usage today:

Pushtu _____ Sanskrit _____

Mongolian _____ Tibetan _____

Latin	_____	Accadian	_____
Aramaic	_____	Coptic	_____
Greek	_____	Phoenician	_____
Norwegian	_____	Syriac	_____

8. What is the syntactic classification of each L: SVO, VOS, etc?

Arabic _____ English _____ French _____
Irish _____ Turkish _____ Japanese _____

CHAPTER 8

LANGUAGE AND COMMUNITY

The speakers of any language do not speak their language in the same way. They are naturally affected by geographical, economic, cultural, and social factors. Further, there are differences among individual speakers caused by the factors of age, sex, education, and profession. As a result of this complicated net of factors, a very wide variety of dialects come into being. These dialects are discussed under a branch of linguistics called sociolinguistics.

Geographical Dialects

As people speaking the same language spread over a Wide Geographical area, Dialects differences among them increase. The larger the Geographical distance between two groups of the same language community is, the greater the **inter- Dialects differences** will be. Dialects that characterize certain regions are called regional or geographical dialects.

These **regional dialects** are caused and enhanced by a variety of reasons. First, different regions have different language contacts determined by bordering foreign communities. The border contacts of the English people, for example, differ from the border contacts of Americans, Australians, or Canadians. That is partly why each people has a distinct dialect. Second, if a group of people is geographical isolated behind a natural barrier such as mountains, deserts, or oceans or by a political barrier , such as blocked borders, this situation will intensify dialectal differences between isolated groups.

In fact, every language has its own main geographical dialects. Every main dialect, further, develops into minor sub- dialects. For instance, English has the variety of British English, American English, Black English, Arab English, Indian English, and many others. American English, for example, has the eastern dialect, the midland dialect, and the western dialect. Each of these dialects has sub- dialects that keep on narrowing down until they reach the town-dialect level.

Social Dialects

People differ as to their social, economic, and educational status . Such factors certainly influence the person's dialect. If you listen well, you can easily see the difference between an educated man's dialect and an illiterate man's dialect. A professor's dialect is surely different from a miner's dialect. The speaker's educational level is a basic factor here, resulting in the determination of the level and type of social companionship. Who you are determines with whom you socialize. So do your economic status and social status. People belonging to the same **socio-economic group** tend to form a distinct social dialect since they differ from other social groups, which develop their own distinct social Dialects

Individual Dialects

Lets us assume that two individuals belong to the same region, live in the same city and even the same street, belong to the same family, and have the same socio-economic status. Nevertheless, their individual dialects will inevitably be different.

Everyone speaks his native or foreign language in a unique manner that distinguishes him from any other speaker. This unique manner is called an **idiolect**. A language like English spoken natively by about five hundred million people has, in fact, 500 million distinct idiolects. No two persons speak a language in exactly the same way.

Every idiolect is characterized by some physical features dependent on the physiology of the speaker's vocal system. That is why we can often identify a person upon merely hearing him, without seeing him. There are certain speech characteristics peculiar to every speaker.

Racial Dialects

A racial minority living among a language majority develop their own dialect, which is the outcome of the interaction between two languages : the first language of the minority (L1) and the second language (L2), i.e., the language of the majority.

Such interaction brings about L3, a new dialect of L2. In the USA, the Blacks have their own dialect, called **Black English** or the English of the Blacks. Turks in Germany, for example, have developed Turkish German, a dialect resulting from German influenced by Turkish. In countries with a lot of immigrants, like the USA, there are dozens of racial dialects : every immigrant minority develops a special racial dialect , e.g., Japanese English, Mexican English, and Vietnamese English.

Professional Dialects

Every Profession has its own **jargon**, i.e., Professional dialect, a dialect with its unique terminology. Engineers, for instance, use terms not used by physicians, agriculturists, lawyers, or accountants. Each jargon has its own lexicon or vocabulary.

Age Dialects

Observe how a three-year child speaks his own native language and what he does to its phonemes, morphology, syntax, lexicon, or semantics. A **child dialect** differs greatly from an **adult dialect**; it differs in all linguistic aspects. The child is still in the learning process, which depends on continual imitation, generalization, hypothesizing, and re-hypothesizing until his dialect matures into an adult .

Sex Dialect

Men have their own dialects, and so do women . A

manly dialect differs from a **womanly dialect** in the performance manner, paralinguistics , i.e., movements accompanying language, voice pitch, some words, some interjections, and some other related factors. This area, in fact , needs further comparative research waiting to be conducted by interested researchers.

Temporal Dialects

Language changes through time especially when influenced by major factors such as long-term foreign occupation, massive immigration, and influential contacts. English, for example , began as Old English (OE), which develop into Middle English (ME), which in turn develop into Modern English. Some dialects simply disappear and are thus labeled as **extinct dialects** like OE and ME.

Rule and Urban Dialects

The same regional dialect divides itself into two sub-dialects : a **rural sub-dialect** for the country and an **urban sub-dialect** for the cities. This sub-division can be traced back to two possible factors. First, a city tends to function as a melting pot of all surrounding villages. Second, urban dwellers are usually more educated and more well-off than Villagers, which controls contribute to the dialectal difference between urban and rural areas.

Colloquial and Standard Dialects

Every language normally shows itself in two major

varieties : standard and colloquial. The **standard dialect** (SD) is that of science , literature, formal writing, university lectures, and dignified speeches. The **colloquial dialect** (CD) is spoken at home, streets, and where the SD is not used. The CD is characterized by its short sentences, simple structures, and frequent vocabulary, unlike the SD.

In fact, the SD and the CD are in **complementary distribution**: one is used where the other cannot be used. The degree of difference, however ,between the SD and the CD varies from a language to another.

Inter-dialectal Differences

Dialects of the same language differ in several aspects:

1. **Phonetic differences**. Taking British English (BE) and American English (AE) as an example, one can consider how these words are pronounced differently in BE and AE: *pass, aunt ,radio ,hot ,*and *letter.*

2. **Syantactic differences**. Some dialects develop Differences in syntax. For example, BE uses *will* and *shall*, whereas AE tends to use *will*. BE uses *haven't* and *hasn't* , whereas AE uses *don't have* and *doesn't have.*

3. **Lexical differences**. BE and AE use these words respectively: *rector /president of a university, flat/apartment, autumn/fall, railway/railroad, public school /private school, minister / secretary, staff/ faculty, mutton /lamb, goods van/freight car, telly /TV, lift/elevator ,headmaster/principal, subway/tube,* and *storey/floor.*

4. **Intonation differences.** Sometimes a dialect has intonation patterns different from those of other dialects. Arabic dialects prove the point obviously and easily, and so do BE and AE.

5. **Spelling differences**. BE and AE differ in spelling too as these respective examples show: *colour/ color, metre/meter, programme/program, labelled / labeled, travelled/traveled, behaviour/ behavior*

Language Taboos

Every community imposes on its members certain verbal restrictions similar to its restrictions on non-verbal behavior. As some acts are disliked, so are some words, which are called language taboos. Therefore , speakers go around such taboos by using metaphors and euphemisms.

Language Types

Being influenced by language conflicts, roles in a community, invasions, immigrations, wars, time, and needs of people, language shows itself in a variety of shapes. A language may be alive, extinct, or semi-alive. An **extinct language**, although once alive, is now dead, e.g., Phoenician, Aramaic, Sanskrit, and Pharonic. A **semi-alive language** is one not used in every life, and its usage is restricted to some occasions only, e.g., Latin, used today in some church sermons only.

A language may be the **first language** (1), the second language (L2), or a **foreign language** (FL). For an Arab,

Arabic is his L1, which he learns first from parents at home through mimicry and **reinforcement**. L1 is the first language which a child hears and learns. If an Arab immigrates to the USA, for instance, English becomes his L2, used side by side with Arabic, his L1. However, for an Arab learning English in class in his own Arab country, English in this case function as a FL.

If a person knows two or three languages, he usually thinks with one of them, not necessarily L1. His **language of thinking** is usually the **dominant language**, the one that he masters best.

In a country of many languages and many minorities, a unified language is chosen to be the **instructional language,** i.e., the language of teaching. In some schools or countries, education is run in two languages; such education is called **bilingual education,** where some school subjects are taught in one L and the others in the other L.

If a country is multi-racial and thus **multi-lingual**, the political will and social needs often require assigning a common language used by all, e.g., English in Australia, Russian in Russia, Chinese in China, and Arabic in any Arab country. Similarly, the multi-lingual country needs an official language (OL) to be used in ministries and official documentation and correspondence. This official language could be the most common language in a country, a policy adopted by Tanzania choosing Swahili, by the Philippines choosing Philippinian , and by Malaysia choosing Malay. However, the **official language**, in some cases, could be an external language, i.e., a language not spoken as first by any local group, to avoid internal political conflicts and protests. Such a policy was adopted by countries like Ghana and Zambia, which chose English as an OL, and by Chad, Gabo, and Senegal, which chose French to be their OL.

Through the process of language formation, a language may be self-dependent in its lexical structure. Such languages are labeled **pure languages** despite the fact that absolute purity is impossible because no language can wholly avoid lexical borrowing from other languages. On the other hand, some languages heavily depend on others in their lexical build-up in a manner beyond normal borrowing. Such languages are called **hybrid languages,** e.g., English, which is a mixture of middle English, French, and Latin, and Urdu, which is a mixture of Hindi, Persian, and Arabic.

In the international arena, languages actually go into combat for dominance. Some of them remain national or local; some prove to be international , i.e., know beyond borders. For example, Albanian has remained within Albania; Romanian, within Romania. In contrast, languages such as English, French, Russian, and Arabic have crossed their national borders and spread in wide areas throughout the world. Nowadays, English, is the dominant **international language**. It has become the language of international business and diplomacy. The internationality of a language is strongly associated with its people's political, economic, and military power. As it is often cited, a language travels with the flag. English, for example, spread where the British army camped; do did French.

Converser's Roles

When two individuals converse, the quality of their conversation is mainly determined by the type of relation they have. Is it a father-son, husband-wife, employer-employee, friend-friend , or colleague relationship? The way one converses with his son is not the same as conversing with his parent, boss, mate, or friend. This relationship often determines the topic of discourse, to begin with. Topics discussable with a friend differ from those Discussable with the bass or a parent. Second, the relationship determines the tone and loudness of voice. Third, the relationship controls the physical distance between the Conversers or between the speaker and the hearer. The more formal a relation is, the larger the distance is. With more and more intimacy, the distance between conversers becomes less and less. Of course, the distance average tends to differ from people to people; in Europe and America, the distance tends to be obviously larger than it is in the Arab world.

Language Interference

When two languages interact within an individual during linguistic performance in speech and writing, each language (L) interferes in the other, with the more dominant L exercising more influence than the less dominant L. This interferes covers all language aspects :morphology, phonetics , syntax, and semantics. L1 colors L2 and L2 colors L1 in the bilingual's mind.

If two communicates with two different languages Intermingle together in the melting pot of everyday life, each community will start learning the other's L; **interference** will begin, and L3 will result as an output of L1-L2 interaction. As intermingling of communities influences their clothes, foods, and customs, so does it certainly influence their languages, depending on duration and magnitude. What applies to languages applies to dialects (D) as well. When D1 interacts with D2 through direct contact of speakers, D3 is going to be formed.

Bilingualism and Community

In some communicates, most individual are **bilinguals,** i.e., persons who use two languages. When we consider the effect of **bilingualism** (B) on the community, we call such B societal B. **Societal B** deals with the effect of B on society with regard to political, social, and demographic aspects.

Societal B handles questions such as dominant L, majority L, minority L, official L, media L, instructional L, and educational policies. Societal B may be one of three types:

1. **Horizontal B**. Two L's are equal in official, social, and culture status in a certain country, e.g., English and French in Quebec in Canada.

2. **Vertical B**. A dialect is a standard one, and another is a colloquial one, as is the case with Arabic in Arab countries. Such B is also called bidialectalism or **diglossia**.

3. **Diagonal B**. Here a country uses a standard dialect (SD) of L1 and a colloquial dialect (CD) of L2,e.g., the SD of English and CD of French in Liousana in the USA.

Bilingualism and Distribution

Sometimes people use L1 and L2 interchangeably anywhere and any time, it is called **reciprocal bilingualism.** In contrast, L1 is used where L2 is not; such B is called **complementary B**. For example, L1 is used at home only, and L2 elsewhere. L1 may be used with some topics and subjects, and L2 with the others. L1 may be used in communicating with some individuals, and L2 with the others.

There are , in fact, many other kinds of B. First, there is **home B**, where two L's are used at home. Second, there is **school B**, where two L's are used in teaching the same student. Third, there is **media B**, where media used two L's to satisfy racial minorities. Fourth, there is **official B**, where all official activities are run in two L's. Fifth, there is **business B**, where employees used and hear two L's at work. Finally, there is **street B**, where two L's are used in streets, cafes, shops, and clubs.

Societal Bilingualism

In some communities, the minority cars to know the majority's L1, whereas the majority does not care to know the majority's L2. In such a case, the minority knows L1 and L2, whereas the majority knows L1 only. This societal bilingualism (SB) is called **one-way** **SB**. For example, the Vietnamese minority in the USA know both English and Vietnamese, whereas the majority does not care to know Vietnamese.

In contrast, some communities have two equally important groups living in linguistic-cultural tolerance and peaceful co-existence. Here each group, out of mutual interest and respect, does use the other group's language. Such SB is called **two-way SB**.

As for the stability of SB in a certain country, it sometimes happens that a country is socially, politically, and administratively stable, and every individual knows which L to use where and when. Such SB is called **stable SB**. On the other hand, a country may change its language policy for some reason, which makes such SB unstable.

This SB non-stability may show itself in two forms. First , the government may facilitate and encourage SB through more language-tolerance procedures in schooling and medial, a case of **progressive SB**. Second, the government may discourage SB and issue legislations favoring monolingualism rather than bilingualism, resulting in a decrease in the number of bilinguals, a case of **regressive SB**.

Language selection

If you know two L's, which L do you select in a certain communicative situation? How and why do you select a certain L and not the other?

There are several factors at work in language selection. First, a person tends to select the L which he is abler at. Next, the speaker tends. If he has the choice, to use the L that the hearer knows better. If the speaker is a new immigrant in a new country, he tends to prefer L1 especially if he is an elderly person proud of his origin, but he tends to use L2 if he belongs to a younger generation so as to show his belongingness to the new home.

Sometimes a bilingual selects the L that gives him better prestige. A person may select a certain L such as English or French to acquire the Prestige associated with that L. It also happens that two persons use L1 at first and use L2 later when their relation gets closer and stronger.

In some cases, the members of a minority select L1 when they converse together and L2 when they converse with people outside the minority. Sometimes social pressure channels the selection of L1 or L2. If a language is hated, its speakers are pressured not to use it in public: its usage becomes rather confidential. In some other cases, the place determines L selection if it is a case of complementary bilingualism: L1, for example, is spoken at home, and L2 elsewhere.

Language Switch

Once a speaker selects the L that he prefers to use in a certain situation, he may code-switch to another L for different reasons or motives. He may wish to prove his mastery of another L. He may see that he can express a certain concept better in L2. He may switch just tentavily: he quotes from L2 and then goes back to L1 or vice versa. He may switch to address a certain person or group of persons who know the switched-to L better.

The speaker may also switch to impress the hearer and come closer to him, implying that they both belong to a certain common racial group. The switch may, moreover, decrease the degree of formality. A switch to L1 or L2 may mean a touch of fun or a touch of seriousness. In addition, a switch may occur when the speaker wants to exclude one hearer and include another .

Code-switching is an interesting behavior that needs further investigation. It may happen inside the sentence, hence called **internal switch**, or outside the sentence, i.e., at sentence borders , hence called **external switch**. In both cases, the switch has rules called **switching rules**, the details of which have no place here in such an introductory book.

Questions and Exercises

(8)

1. What kind of dialect is each following one: a geographical, social, racial, individual, professional, age, sex, or temporal dialect?

American English   _____   idolect   _____

Black English   _____   child dialect   _____

Middle English   _____   manly dialect   _____

doctor's jargon   _____   Turkish German   _____

Indian English   _____   Canadian English   _____

Lebanese Arabic   _____   adult dialect   _____

2. Define these terms:

a. L1:_____

_____

b. L2:_____

_____

c. FL:_____

_____

3. Give the British synonym of each following American word. Example: elevator/lift.

principal   _____   floor   _____

fall   _____   apartment   _____

tube   _____   lamb   _____

4. Define these terms:

a. bilingualism: _____

_____

b. multilingualism: _____

_____

c. language taboo: _____

_____

d. language interference: _____

_____

e. diglossia: _____

_____

5. What kind of bilingualism does each following case represent?

a. Two languages are used equally in a community. _____

b. Two dialects of the same language are used in a country. _____

c. L1 is used at home, and L2 elsewhere. _____

d. Two L's are used at home. _____

e. The TV and radio use two L's. _____

f. Two ethnic groups use one another's L in addition to their own L.

g. The number of bilinguals is decreasing in a certain country. _____

h. A country encourages bilingualism, and the number of bilinguals is rising continually. _____

i. The state policy towards bilingualism is not clear and keeps on changing. _____

j. School subjects are taught in two languages. _____

6. An Arab learner of English made these errors. What kind of interference from Arabic led to each error: phonetic, morphological, syntactic, or semantic? Why did it occur?

a. * This is the man whom I saw him yesterday. _____

Why?_____
b.* You can do it, isn't it?   _____
Why?_____
c. * The apple sweet.   _____
Why?_____
d. * The boys they are present.   _____
Why?_____
e. * Look at the flower the beautiful.   _____
Why?_____

7. Thee are pronunciation errors made by an Arab learning English. Explain how interference from Arabic could be the cause of such errors.

a. He pronounced *street* as /sitriyt/ instead of / sitriyt/ .

_____

b. He pronounced *peg* as /big/ instead of /big/ .

_____

c. He pronounced /v/ *in university* as /f/ .

_____

d. He doubled the pronunciation of double letters in *collect*, *connect*, and *arrange*.

_____

159

CHAPTER 9

WRITING

Writing is a secondary and incomplete representation of speech. Normal orthography does not represent speech fully due to these reasons:

1. Speech shows pitch, unshown in writing.
2. Speech shows the emotional mood of the speaker such as happiness , anger, sadness, pain, or repentance, whereas emotion are not shown in writing except lexically.
3. Speech is accompanied and supplemented by facial expressions, nonexistent in writing.
4. Speech is accompanied and supplemented by body movements, unshown in writing.
5. Speech has stress and intonation contours, absent in writing.

Development of Writing

Inscriptions and antique writings show that human writing passed through a series of developmental stages:

1. **Ideography** or idea writing. Writing started as drawings not linked to a certain language. The limitation of this technique is that only a few people had or has the ability to draw. Even if that could, the same drawing could be interpreted differently by different decoders. Further, the

same idea might be drawn in different ways, a matter which adds to confusion in both encoding and decoding.

2. **Logography**. In ideography, the symbol stands for an idea. Here, in logography, the symbol stands for a word, one step forward towards more preciseness.

3. **Syllabic writing.** Here , the symbol stands for one syllable, a method still used by some languages such as Japanese.

4. **Alphabetic writing**. Here comes the most precise writing system, where one symbol is to stand for one phoneme. It is believe that ancient Egyptians were the initiators of alphabetic writing, and the oldest alphabetic inscriptions go back to B.C. 1725 left by Phoenicians in Ancient Lebanon. Then the alphabet was developed by different peoples into the different systems now in use.

Direction of writing

Not all languages are written or read in the same direction. Arabic, as is known, is written and read from right to left. English goes from left to right. Japanese goes from the top to the bottom . Semitic languages behave like Arabic; European languages behave like English.

Types of Writing

The alphabetic writing dominantly used nowadays is of various types. The first type is the normal **orthographic**

writing, which we use when we write and which you see on this page before your eyes now . In normal writing, letters usually, but not consistently, stand for phonemes. In some language , like Arabic, each letter stands for one phoneme and each phoneme is represented by one letter.

However , in some other languages, letters do not correspond perfectly to phonemes, a phenomenon called **imperfect fit**: graphemes do not always parallel phonemes. Such is English , where *ghoti*, strangely enough, may be read *fish* since *gh* in *enough* is /f/, *o* in *women* is /i/, and *ti* in *dictation* is / š /

Another type of writing is **phonemic writing**, where a word is written in phonemes, not in graphemes, as it is exactly pronounced: /d a g/ for *dog*, /hæt/ for *hat*, / ðis / for *this,* /rayt/ for *write*, /leyt/ for *late*, /nayf/ for *knife*, and so on. The phonemic symbols appearing here are supposed to be used to phonemically write all languages since these symbols are devised by IPA, the International Phonetic Association.

A third type of writing is phonetic **writing**, which uses IPA symbols as phonemic writing does and adds to them certain diacritics that mark secondary phonetic features such as aspiration, nasalization, devoicing, verlarization, non-release, e.g., [p¹it⁻],[sp⁼in], where [p¹] stands for aspiration, [t⁻] for non-release, and [p⁼] for non-aspiration.

Notice these symbols. We use < > to include normal writing, slashes / / for phonemic writing, and square brackets [   ] for phonetic writing. Among the three types, phonetic writing is the most precise one and the most representative of speech since it represents phonemes and their additional phonetic features as well.

Phonemic-Graphemic Differences

With more differences between the phonemic form and the graphemic form of a language, more spelling problems are anticipated to arise. In the case of English, even native speakers find some difficulties with spelling owing to the fact that English is written differently from how it is pronounced in many cases.

Some there are **regular patterns**, however. Look at these groups which follow patternized form:

1. *fin, sit, win, bit, kit.*
2. *fine, site, wine, bite, kite.*
3. *fat, rat, hat, mat.*
4. *fate, rate, hate, mate.*

On the other hand look at these words, and see the difference between how they are written and how they are pronounced : *knight, circle, book, chronic, digs, wished, author, capable, these, fur, success, lives, syllables, ideas, people, now, know, or, her, can , enough, photo, one, reason.* You cannot pronounce any of these words correctly if you pronounce it as it is written. **Reading pronunciation**, i.e., saying as you see, in most cases, gives a wrong pronunciation in English.

Therefore, as has been demonstrated, the imperfect fit results in two inseparable problems. First, there is a problem in spelling: you cannot spell correctly if you wholly depend on what you hear. Second, there is a problem in pronunciation: you cannot pronounce correctly if you wholly depend on what you see.

Consonantal Writing

Some languages choose to include consonants and long vowels in normal writing and exclude short vowels. Such writing is called **consonantal writing**. An example of such language is Arabic. However, if written Arabic is vocalized, all segmental phonemes ,i.e., consonants and vowels , appear, and, therefore, Arabic **vocalized writing** is almost perfect.

Pronunciation Rules

Although English writing does not match English pronunciation very well. There are some rules that organize the relationship between writing and pronunciation. Here are some of them.

1. If the plurality <s> comes after a voiceless final sound, it is pronounced /s/, e.g., *cats, pipes.*
2. If the plurality <s> comes after a voiced final sound, it is /z/, e.g., *doors, heads.*

3. If the plurality <s> comes after a hissing sound, it is / ɨ z /,e.g., *churches, buses, images.*

4. The same three previous rules apply to the <s> added to the verb, e.g., *takes, goes, washes.*

5. The same three rules apply to the possessive <s>, e.g., *Jack's hat, John's hat, James's hat.*

6. The same three rules apply to the contracted <s>, which means *is* or *has*, e.g., *Jack come, John's here, James's gone.*

7. The past <d> after a voiceless final sound is /t/, e.g., *kicked, kissed, topped.*

8. The past <d> after a voiced final sound is /d/, e.g., *feared, learned, sealed.*

9. The past <d> after a final /t/ or /d/ is / ɪd / ,e.g., *wanted, demanded.*

10. If <st> is medial, /t/ is often zero , e.g., *fasten, listen, whistle, glisten, castle, hasten.*

11. <k> initial before /n/ is often zero, e.g., *knife, knight, Kneel.*

12. <w> initial before /h/ or /r/ is sometimes zero, e.g., *who, whole, wrong.*

13. <h> before <0> is often zero, e.g., *honorary, hour, honest.*

14. <h> after /w/ is often zero, e.g., *why, when, what.*

15. <1> before a consonant and after a vowel is often zero, e.g., *chalk, half, could, walk.*

16. A final <e> often makes <a, I, o> pronounced as they are named, and the final /e/ is zero, e.g., *hate, late, bite, fine, note, robe.*

17. /b/ final after /m/ is zero, e.g., comb, womb, thumb, climb.

18. A doubled letter is just one phoneme, e.g., *common, affect* and *better*, with the exception of prefixes, e.g., *dissatisfied.*

19. <g> is /g/ if followed by a consonant or <o,u,a>, e.g., *great, go, gun, game.*

20. <g> is /ǰ/ if final before silent < e > or often so if before <e,i>, e.g., *change, general, original.*

21. <g> before final /n/ is zero, e.g., *sign, foreign, assign.*
22. <c> before <i , e> is /s/, e.g., *city, cell.* Otherwise, it Is /k/, e.g., *carry, country, cut, close.*

23. <c> after /s/ is often zero , e.g., *muscle, scent, scientific.*
24. <c> before /k/ is often zero, e.g., *neck , back, black.*
25. Final <re> in British English is / ə r /, e.g., *theatre, centre.* In American English, it is written <e r>,e.g., *theater center.*

166

26. The article <the> is / ð ə / before a consonant and / ðe / before a vowel, e.g., *the book, the apple.*

Spelling Rules

The imperfect fit between English graphemes and English phonemes causes a lot of spelling problems in addition to pronunciation problems. However, there are some rules that may control and organize spelling:

1. If a final <e> is followed by a suffix beginning with a vowel, it is usually omitted, e.g., *write + ing* → *writing, desire + able* → *desirable.*

2. If the final letters are <ee> and a suffix is added, nothing is omitted, e.g., *see + able* → *seeable, agree + able* → *agreeable.*

3. If the final is <e> and a suffix beginning with a consonant is added, the final <e> is not usually omitted, e.g., *move + ment* → *movement, hate + ful* → *hateful.*

4. Some exceptions to the previous rules are *mileage, acreage, noticeable*, and *changeable.*

5. To mark the possessive (genitive) case, add'*s* to the singular, e.g., *boy's, Mary's.*

6. If the noun is plural without a final –s, add'*s* to make the possessive, e.g., *women's, men's.*

7. If the noun is a proper noun ending in <s>, '*s* or '

only may be added to make the possessive, e.g., *James's* or *James'*, preferably the first choice.

8. Pronouns do not take 's or 'for the possessive. The exceptions are indefinite pronouns, e.g., *someone's, one's.*

9. Some abbreviations in spelling are *he's (=he has, he is), we're (=we are), I'm (= I am), sh'd (= she would, she had), they've (= they have).*

10. A final <y> is changed into <i> if preceded by a consonant and a suffix beginning with a vowel is added , e.g., *country + es → countries , carry + ed → carried.*

11. If the final <y> is preceded by a vowel and a suffix beginning with a vowel is added, no change takes place, e.g., *pray + ed → prayed.*

12. Rule 10 does not apply if the suffix begins with <i>, e.g., *carry + ing → carrying.* The letter <y> remains as it is in this case.

13. A proper noun ending in –y is pluralized by adding <s> regardless of what precedes <y>, e.g., *Marys, Nancys, Mays*

14. If a final consonant is preceded by a stressed short simple vowel and a suffix beginning with a vowel is added, the consonant is doubled, e.g., *drop + ed → dropped, run + ing → running.*

15. If the final letter is <c>, it is doubled by adding /k/ upon applying Rule 14, e.g., *traffic + ed → trafficked.*

16. Generally , <i> is before <e> except after <c> ,e. g., *niece, belief, receive*, when pronounced as /iy/

17. With verbs ending in <ie>, change <ie> into <y> before adding <ing>, e.g., *tie + ing → tying, lie + ing → lying.*

Questions and Exercises
(9)

1. What is the last phoneme in each word? Is it /s/, /z/, or / iz /?

hoofs	_____	amounts	_____
virtues	_____	views	_____
languages	_____	walks	_____
countries	_____	speakers	_____
linguists	_____	describes	_____
Robert's	_____	differs	_____
Mary 's	_____	she's	_____
facts	_____	hips	_____
courses	_____	rights	_____
fines	_____	fits	_____
kits	_____	fails	_____
uses	_____	drives	_____
suffixes	_____	affects	_____
washes	_____	forests	_____
Thomas's	_____	Hoop's	_____
illustrations	_____	Edward's	_____
others	_____	brides	_____
roots	_____	values	_____
kids	_____	files	_____
lips	_____	establishes	_____
closes	_____	talks	_____
Bob's	_____	he's	_____
acts	_____	digs	_____

2. Is the last phoneme in these words /t/ ,/d/, / ɪd /?

separated	_____	labeled	_____
tried	_____	interpreted	_____
quoted	_____	pronounced	_____
analyzed	_____	informed	_____
commanded	_____	uttered	_____
sounded	_____	operated	_____
traced	_____	reflected	_____
laughed	_____	wished	_____
lived	_____	stripped	_____
visualized	_____	silenced	_____
described	_____	halfed	_____
submitted	_____	voiced	_____
rested	_____	picked	_____
enjoyed	_____	engaged	_____
looked	_____	guided	_____
expressed	_____	ranged	_____
originated	_____	suppressed	_____
differed	_____	seemed	_____
observed	_____	jumped	_____
used	_____	shipped	_____
confused	_____	realized	_____
adopted	_____	derived	_____
watched	_____	kicked	_____

3. Underline any zero phonemes in these words, i.e., not pronounced , and mention the reason. Examples: *resign*, before final /n/ .

castle	_____	mustn't	_____
knee	_____	knob	_____
wrap	_____	wreck	_____

knock	_____	know	_____
whale	_____	whisper	_____
folk	_____	half	_____
tomb	_____	autumn	_____
hour	_____	where	_____
should	_____	pipe	_____
dumb	_____	lamb	_____
condemn	_____	column	_____

4. Is \<g\> in these words pronounced /g/, / ʒ /, or zero? Why?

gut	_____	figure	_____
disgust	_____	page	_____
genius	_____	huge	_____
assign	_____	resignation	_____
glove	_____	gold	_____
grammar	_____	tragic	_____
tongue	_____	tag	_____
fog	_____	grand	_____
design	_____	grind	_____
grim	_____	single	_____
feeling	_____	suggest	_____
foreign	_____	range	_____

5. Is \<c\> pronounced /s/ , /k/, or zero? Why?

physical	_____	stuck	_____
scenario	_____	civilization	_____
combine	_____	restricted	_____
close	_____	stick	_____
completion	_____	per cent	_____
structural	_____	secondary	_____

muscle	_____	captain	_____
decisive	_____	recruit	_____
cone	_____	describe	_____
center	_____	constitute	_____
pack	_____	cassette	_____
voice	_____	direction	_____
conversation	_____	command	_____
precede	_____	practice	_____
conquest	_____	mock	_____

6. Re-write these combinations to make one word in each case:

prove + able	_____	free + able	_____
pronounce + ing	_____	classify + ed	_____
arrange + er	_____	behave + ior	_____
teachers + 's	_____	student + 's	_____
key + s	_____	storey + s	_____
fly + s	_____	Harry + s	_____
swim + er	_____	travel + er	_____
quiz + ed	_____	talk + ing	_____
picnic + ed	_____	rid + ing	_____
ride + ing	_____	hot + est	_____
large + est	_____	listen + er	_____
see + ing	_____	die + ing	_____
buy + er	_____	tray + s	_____
try + s	_____	marry + d	_____
fry + ing	_____	fry + d	_____

CHAPTER 10

LANGUAGE
ACQUISITION

How does an individual acquire a language, whether his first language (L1), second language (L2), or foreign language (FL) ? This question is answered by a branch of applied linguistics called psycholinguistics, which also deals with the individual's language development, how this is related to thinking, brain functions, mental age, intelligence, motivation, and the like.

Influential Factors

There are several factors that affect the acquisition of L1:

1. **Age**. The child must reach a certain age to begin his first sounds, then his first words, and then his first sentences. Brain readiness through time is a basic factor.

2. **Language center**. There is a nervous department in the brain in charge of language encoding and decoding. This center has to be physiologically healthy in order to function properly.

3. **Language environment**. The child has to hear L as a

prerequisite to speaking it. Without an adequate **input**, there will be no satisfactory **output**.

4. **Hearing**. If the child is deaf, he cannot receive L. Consequently. He cannot acquire it.

5. **Sex**. Research has shown that female children acquire L1 earlier than male children. This earlier maturity of females is not restricted to language only, but it extends to physical and mental maturity as well.

6. **Intelligence**. A more intelligent child acquires more vocabulary in a shorter time, and his comprehension is faster and more precise than a less intelligent one.

7. **Physical health**. A physically healthy child is normally in a better position to acquire language than a physically infirm child since infirmity puts pressure on mental activity and functions as a hinderer to L learning.

8. **Bilingualism**. If a child is exposed to two L's at a very early age, this exposure may confuse him and delay his progress with both L1 and L2.

9. **Regressive behavior**. If a child is pressured to speak before optimal age, this overdemanding pressure may give an opposite result. He may refrain from attempting to speak, fearing failure or avoiding parental dissatisfaction.

Role of the Hearing Sense

The ear plays an essential role in language acquisition

(LA). It is the gate which allows L to get directly into the specialized brain center, where the **linguistic input** is decoded, classified, stored, and later retrieved. This center has a sophisticated job related to storing thousands of words, their meanings, usage, spelling, and pronunciation, with thousands of facts about morphology, syntax, and semantics. Add to all this another language or two. It is a real burden shouldered very efficiently by a miraculous small piece of flesh called the brain, or to put it more precisely, by a very narrow area in the brain called the **language center**.

Notice that a child born deaf and remaining so can never acquire L and, thus, becomes dumb. However, if deafness comes later, i.e., some years after birth when the child has already had the opportunity to receive L, he can speak although unable to hear.

Role of the Sight Sense

The eye has a role in L acquisition although it is much less important than the role of the ear. A blind-born child can acquire L, whereas a deaf-born child cannot. The eye, first, observes the movements of **external articulators** such as lips and, thus, helps in sound perception. The eye, by perceiving the environment surrounding the conversational activity, can also help in understanding the speaker's message better and more easily. Further, the eye helps the hearer to see the speaker's body language, which supplements comprehending verbal language.

Moreover, the eye makes seeing the speaker's facial

features and expressions possible. It cannot be forgotten that the eye is essential to the two skills of reading and writing, where the ear has little or no role at all to play.

Language Brain Centers

The brain follows a specialization policy. It is divided into centers, each of which is in charge of a certain assignment. There are a breath center, a heart center, a hearing center, a seeing center, a tasting center, and a smelling center, not to forget language centers, among many other centers in the brain. In fact, the brain has four language centers:

1. **Speech center**. The speech center sends motor orders to articulatorz organs through motor nerves so as to produce the desired language phones. This center gives instructions to the tongue, lips, and other articulators to move in the right time, in the right direction, and to the right place so as to produce every single allophone.

2. **Writing center**. It gives motor orders to manual muscles to write the right graphemes.

3. **Audible-word center**. It receives spoken words through the ears and then decodes verbal messages.

4. **Written-word center**. It perceives written language and then decodes it.

These four centers are located in the left side of the brain, i.e., the **left hemisphere**, in the case of right-handed

people. Normally, the right ear receives spoken L better than the left ear, a phonemenon called **right-ear dominance** (RED). This right-ear left-hemisphere connection is in line with the criss-cross nervous-system pattern of connection.

The theory of language centers finds support in what happens to people after accidents and injuries. The injured person may lose some, not all, of the four L abilities: listening, speaking, reading, and writing. He may lose the speech ability, for instance, but he retains the other three. This proves that each skill is co-ordinated by a specialized center and disproves the hypothesis that all language skills are processed by one single brain center. Had it been otherwise, any damage to the language center would have caused a total loss of all the four language skills.

Circle of Language Contact

Language contact between two persons starts when there is a motive for it. Such a motive may be social, emotional, utilitarian, financial, information-seeking, or the like. With the motive, the will for contact comes to existence. Hence, the brain prepares the message, and, then or meanwhile, it sends orders to the articulation system to begin producing the message. Thus, **language transmission** begins; the hearer receives, and his brain decodes. According to decoding, the hearer's brain selects the proper message and sends it to the speaker. The two persons exchange messages through alternate processes of **encoding** and **decoding**.

When X is the sender, Y is the receiver. When Y takes the sender's role, X takes the receiver's role. The exchange of roles continues until one or both decide to stop the contact.

This conversational contact is an action wholly performed by the brain with its specialized language centers assisted by speech organs, the hearing system, and the sight system. It is the brain that chooses vocabulary, meanings, syntax, and sentences. It also gives orders to the speech systems to orally produce the message. It receives coming oral messages and decodes them as well.

Stages of Language Development

When the infant is born, he knows nothing of any language. Nevertheless, he is born with **innate readiness** to acquire language. The actual acquisition passes through these stages:

1. **Stage of first sounds**. The infant's first cry upon birth is his first sound, which is essential to activating and widening his lungs. Later on, he produces emotional sounds in response to hunger, thirst, pain, or pleasure. Such sounds are non-linguistic sounds common to all children of the world.

2. **Stage of babbling**. In the fourth or fifth month, the child begins babbling, i.e., playing with sounds, as if he is experimenting with his vocal system partly in **imitation** of adults and partly out of curiosity. He probably wants to test

his vocal organs, to entertain himself with his own sounds,

and to please his mother by showing her his vocal ability. The babbling sounds at this stage may be both linguistic and non-linguistic. Nonetheless, the child starts, under the effect of imitation and parental reinforcement, to gradually eliminate non-linguistic sounds, retain, and repeat linguistic ones in a gradual refining process.

3. **Stage of first words**. Words the child is about thirteen months old, he begins to produce his first words, sometimes called word sentences or sentence words, i.e., a sentence of one word or a word standing for a sentence. When the child wants water, he only says the word *water*, and he says it in his own interesting child dialect.

In this stage, the child learns words through thing-word association, compassion, trial-error-omission, and reinforcement. Reinforcement means that he receives an encouraging signal, usually from his mother, such as an approval smile to mark his correct performance and probably another disapproval signal to mark his incorrect performance. Of course, vocabulary learning is a lifelong process although it proceeds very quickly in the Childs early years.

4. **Stage of sentences**. When the child is $\pm$ 24 months old, he begins to form two-word sentences that basically contain content words with the usual exclusion of function words such as prepositions, conjunctions, and articles . He would say *Dad came* or *Dad here*, without the auxiliary *is*. Later on, the sentence gradually becomes longer and longer with more of compound and complex sentences.

Trends of Language Acquisition

As a result of longitudinal and cross-sectional observation of children's language behavior, one may come to these conclusions about the general tendencies of language acquisition (LA):

1. LA goes from the simple to the complex, e.g., sounds, syllables, words, and then sentences.

2. In LA, the child produces external sounds before producing internal ones, e.g., bilabials before velars, because he can observe and learn their production more easily.

3. Noun words are acquired before other words probably owing to their association with concrete things in most cases.

4. Content words are required before function words.

5. Words related to the concrete are acquired before those related to the abstract.

6. Words are understood by the child before they are produced by him.

7. The child prefers short words to long ones out of easiness in storage, recollection, and usage. Hence, his first words tend to be monosyllabic.

8. The meaning of a word in the child's mind may be different from its meaning in the adult's. It may be wider or

narrower, depending on his experience with language and life.

9. First sentences tend to be short. Later, they become longer.

10. The child's first sentences are simple. Later, he develops compound and complex ones.

11. The child prefers easy phones. Difficult ones may be replaced by easier ones.

Theories of Language Acquisition

A child acquires his first language (L1) through a variety of mechanisms as different theories suggest:

1. **Acquisition by imitation**. Some believe that the child acquire L1 mainly through imitating parents, adults, and peers around him. He does this imitation both to get social approval and to express his own needs. However, this theory cannot explain how a child does and can produce sentences which he has never heard.

2. **Acquisition by reinforcement**. Some believe that a child acquires L1 through **positive reinforcement** : he tries correctly and, thus, gets his mother's approval in the form of a smile, a kiss, praise, or a pat. He also acquires L1 through **negative reinforcement**: he tries incorrectly and is, thus, corrected usually by his parents, especially his mother.

3. **Acquisition by innate readiness**. Some believe that

LA takes place because man is created with the innate capacity to acquire language: he is programmed to do so when he reaches the proper age provided that he receives the essential language input through adequate exposure.

4. **Complementary acquisition.** The author holds that no one previous theory can fully account for LA. Imitation alone cannot explain LA. Neither reinforcement nor Innateness alone can. As a matter of fact, each of imitation, reinforcement, and innateness has a basic role in LA.

Second-Language Acquisition

Second language acquisition (L2A) or foreign language acquisition (FLA) is certainly different from acquiring the first language (L1) because motives, situations, and relevant factors are obviously different. L2A or FLA is dependent, with regard to speed and mastery, on several factors; whatever applies to L2 here applies to FL too.

1. **Natural linguistic environment**. To hear L2 in a natural environment is better than hearing it in an artificial environment such as a classroom.

2. **Learner's role.** The more the learner of L2 or FL participates activity in conversational situations, the better the learning situation is.

3. **Using concretes**. If L2 is associated with concretes, learning would be more natural, real, and motivating.

4. **Language model.** All language learning requires a model, i.e., a person to be imitated by the learner. The more the model mastersL2, the better he is for the learner.

5. Feedback. The L2 learner needs some feedback to know whether his performance is right or wrong. **Immediate feedback** is better than delayed feedback: the sooner, the better. Positive feedback is better than negative feedback: to reward is better than to punish. Selective feedback is better than comprehensive feedback: correcting some errors is better than error hunting, i.e., correcting all errors.

6. Repetition. The more the learner hears a word or a pattern, the faster he learns it, and the more permanent his learning will be.

7. Quantity of exposure. With more language input, i.e., more exposure to oral and written language in terms of quantity and time, L2A becomes faster, and more support is given to the output.

8. Readiness. Like L1, L2A has an optimal age. To avoid damaging L1A (first language acquisition), the best age for L2A is ± 11, i.e., about the age of eleven years.

9. Motivation. There is no learning without attention, and there is no attention without motivation. The motive for L2A may be academic success, belonging to a new country or nation or religion, obtaining a prize, tourism, or business. The motive may be **internal** or external, **permanent** or tentative. Internal and permanent motives are stronger and more conducive to L2A than external and tentative ones.

10. Relaxation. If L2 is learned in a psychologically healthy and socially comfortable situation, L2A will be faster.

11. **Anxiety**. A little anxiety on the learner's side stimulates him to learn. Nonetheless, over- anxiety hinders L2A.

12. **Self-confidence**. Self-trust encourages the L2 learner to try producing the language with minimal or no hesitation, away from shyness or embarrassment.

13. **Character.** An extrovert tends to be a faster L2 learner than an introvert partly because the former is more sociable by definition: he likes to interact and talk to other people.

14. **Age**. Children are better than adults in imitation, and adults are better in the areas of general experience, language analysis, comprehension, and memory.

15. **Transfer**. Where L1 and L2 are similar, L1 facilities L2A, and this is called **positive transfer**. Where L1 and L2 are different, L1 hinders L2A, and this is called **negative transfer**. With more and more L1-L2 similarities, L2A is fortunately made easier.

16. **Attitude.** A learner may like or dislike L2 because he likes or dislikes its people, i.e., its native speakers. This emotional attitude is dependent on historical and political relations. It may be difficult for a person to like a country

that took part in aggression, war, occupation, or bombardment of his own country - let alone liking the language of that country. In contrast, a positive attitude towards a country and its language places the learner in a better emotional position with regard to L2A or FLA.

Differences between L1A and FLA

There are significant differences between first-language acquisition (L1A), i.e., acquiring mother tongue, and foreign-language acquisition (FLA). Here are some of these differences:

1. **Motive**. With L1, the motive of the learner is very much stronger than with FL. He needs L1 to satisfy his basic needs such as needs for water and food.

2. **Environment**. With L1, the language environment is natural, whereas it is artificial with FL.

3. **Practice.** With L1, the child hears and produces the language for about sixteen hours daily. With FL, he has the maximum of one hour daily at school.

4. **Reinforcement**. With L1, the child is probably the only learner in his mother's class; therefore, he receives frequent and immediate feedback from his mother almost whenever he says anything. With FL, reinforcement is comparatively very much less.

5. **Ease**. With L1, the child is at full ease, close to dear mother. With FL, there is, not unlikely, the uncomfortable pressure of the teacher , peers, and classroom competition

and embarrassment.

6. **Age**. With L1, the age of language learning, i.e., early childhood, is always optimally appropriate. With FL, which may start at any age, that age may not always be as appropriate as it is with L1.

7. **Interference**. With L1, no other language is interfering simply because there is no other language to interfere. With FL, there is L1 always ready to interfere.

8. **Feelings**. With L1, the learner's feelings are invariably positive since L1 is the language of the people whom he loves. With FL, his feelings might be positive ,negative , or mixed. He looks at the FL as a school subject, which he may like or dislike.

Linguistic Interference

When an individual learns FL or L2, he undergoes interference coming from L1. As it is known, interference goes from the more **dominant L** to the less dominant L. Normally, L1 is more dominant and therefore, interference often moves from L1 to L2 or FL. This interference is always negative and is, therefore, sometimes called **negative transfer.**

Language interference shows itself in different aspects. First, it may be a **phonetic interference**, where some L1

phonemes damage some L2 phonemes. For example, an Arab learning English may say /i/ instead of /e/ because Arabic does not have /e/ . Second, it may be a **morphological**

interference. The learner of L2, for instance, may pluralize some L2 nouns in wrong analogy with some L1 nouns. Third, it may be a **lexical interference**, where L1 words move into L2 lexicon with the same or different meanings. Fourth, it may be a **syntactic interference**. For example, an Arab may wrongly omit the verb from the English sentence because Arabic allows such omission in nominal verbless sentences. Fifth, it may be a **semantic interference**, where L1 meanings are wrongly imposed on L2 meanings. Sixth, it may be a **kinetic interference**, where a learner of L2 uses, with L2, body movements that he usually uses with L1.

Bilingual Brain

The bilingual brain is the brain of a bilingual person, i.e., a person who knows two languages. The pertinent question here is this: How does the bilingual brain store and process the two language? There are two hypotheses with this regard. The first hypothesis is the **common-storage hypothesis**: there is one mental dictionary for both L1 and L2, but this dictionary labels every language component as either L1 or L2 so as to facilitate the process of retrieval during comprehension and expression. The second hypothesis is the **independent-storage hypothesis**. According to this second theory, there are two mental dictionaries: one for L1 and the other for L2. Each hypothesis has its proponents, proofs, and experiments, the details of which certainly have no place here.

Aphasia of Bilinguals

Because of accidents and subnormal mental cases, some

bilinguals may suffer **aphasia**, i.e., language loss. The inflected person may recover partly or wholly. This recovery may take different forms:

1. **Parallel restriction**. The inflected person retrieves L1 and L2 at the same speed and time.
2. **Unparallel restriction**. He retrieves one language before the other and at different speeds.
3. **Selective restriction**. He retrieves one language and not the other.
4. **Sequential restriction**. He retrieves one language after he completes the retrieval of the other.
5. **Alternate restrictions**. When L1 is retrieved, L2 is forgotten. When L2 is remembered, L1 is forgotten.
6. **Confused restriction**. The two languages are restored mixed together during speaking and writing.

To interpret and account for these different types of restriction, specialists have proposed various hypotheses:

1. **Order hypothesis**. One remembers first the language that he acquired first.
2. **Usage hypothesis**. One recalls first language that he uses more frequently .
3. **Mood hypothesis**. If the afflicted person was satisfied, before aphasia, with a person speaking a certain language, he tends to recall this language before the other one.

4. **Exposure hypothesis**. The afflicted person tends to restore first the language that he hears more during his aphasia period from his visitors, doctors, and nurses.

5. **Mastery hypothesis**. The aphasia-afflicted person tends to restore first the language that he masters more.

Language Lateralization

Research has shown that right-handed monolinguals store language in the **left hemisphere**, i.e., the left side of the brain. In contrast, left-handed monolinguals store it in the **right hemisphere**. These facts have been categorically proven by the results of brain surgery. When the right hemispheres of some monolingual patients were surgically eliminated, their language performance was not damaged. But when the left hemisphere was eliminated, linguistically they could perform nothing. In addition, local anesthesia of brain hemispheres has proven the same conclusions.

Concerning bilinguals, psycholinguists have given different answers concerning language lateralization:

1. Some specialists argue that bilinguals use the right hemisphere of the brain more than monolinguals.

2. Some theories hold that if L2 is required before $\pm$ 11 years of age, language control is centered in the left hemisphere. If after, this control goes to the right hemisphere.

3. Some research conclusions state that at the early

stage of L2 acquisition, the right hemisphere plays an active role. Later, when L2 is mastered, the left hemisphere becomes in complete control.

4. Other theories argue that if L2 is acquired naturally, the right hemisphere has a share larger than that of the left hemisphere. If artificially, the left hemisphere gets the larger share.

5. Some studies have concluded that 80% of people, whether monolingual or not, have their language control in the left hemisphere of the brain.

Questions and Exercises
(10)

A. Define these terms:

1. Babbling Stage: _____

_____

2. Reinforcement: _____

_____

3. Language Model: _____

_____

4. Feedback: _____

_____

5. Language Exposure: _____

_____

6. Positive Transfer: _____

_____

7. Negative Transfer: _____

_____

8. Parallel Restitution: _____

_____

9. Selective Restitution: _____

_____

10. Sequential Restitution: _____

B. Decide whether each statement is true or false If false, why?

1. There is one L center in the brain. _____

Why? _____

_____

2. The eye has no role in L acquisition. _____
   Why?_____
   _____

3. L centers are usually located in the right hemisphere of
   The brain.   _____
   Why?_____
   _____

4. The third stage in L acquisition is the stage of sentences.
                                                   _____
   Why?_____
   _____

5. Innate readiness is enough to explain L acquisition.
                                                   _____
   Why?_____
   _____

6. The best age to learn the FL is $\pm$ 16.   _____
   Why?_____
   _____

7. Anxiety always hurts L2 learning.   _____
   Why?_____
   _____

8. With the FL, the child gets more reinforcement than with
   L1.   _____
   Why? _____
   _____

9. When you learn your L1,L2 interferes.   _____
   Why?_____
   _____

10. If one knows L2 more than L1, L1 interferes in L2.
                                                   _____

Why?_____

_____

11. The bilingual has one mental dictionary according to
     the independent-storage hypothesis.   _____
     Why?_____

     _____

12.   Brain surgery supports L-lateralization theory.

                                           _____

     Why?_____

     _____

SELECTED
BIBLIOGRAPHY

Alkhuli, Muhammad Ali. *A Contrastive Transformational Grammar: Arabic and English.* The Hague: Bill, 1980

Anderson, S.R. *The Organization of Phonology*. N.Y.: Academic Press, 1974

Aronoff, M. *Word Formation in Generative Grammar.* Cambridge Mass: MIT Press, 1976

Chomsky, N. *Syntactic Structures.* The Hague: Mouton, 1957.

Comrie, B. (ed). *The World's Major Languages.* N.Y.: Oxford University Press, 1990.

Fodor, J.A., and T.G. Bever. *The Psychology of Language.* N.Y.: Mc Graw-Hill, 1986.

Fromkin, V., and R. Rodman. *An Introduction to Language.* N.Y.: Holt, Rinehart and Winston, 1993.

Hughes, J.R., and B. Heasley. *Semantics.* Cambridge, England: Cambridge University Press, 1993.

Katzner, K. *The Languages of the World.* London: Routeledge & Kegan Paul, 1986.

Ladefoged, P. *A Course in Phonetics.* Fort Worth: Harcourt Brace Jovanovich, 1993.

Lyons, John. *Introduction to Theoretical Linguistics.* London: Cambridge University Press, 1968.

_____ *Semantics*. Cambridge, England: Cambridge Univ. Press, 1977.

Radford, A. *Transformational Grammar*. N.Y.: Cambridge Univ. Press, 1988.

Sled, James. *A Short Introduction to English Grammar*. Chicago: Scott, Foresman & Co., 1975.

Spencer, A. *Morphological Theory*. London: Basil Blackwell, 1991.

Springer, S.P. and G. Deutch. *Left Brain, Right Brian*. San Francisco, Calif: W. H. Freeman, 1981.

Trudgill, P. *Sociolinguistics*. Middlesex, England: Penguin Books, 1977.

Wanner,E. and L. Gleitman (eds). *Language Acquisition*. Cambridge, England: Cambridge Univ. Press, 1982.

APPENDIX I
ABBREVIATIONS

Adj	adjective	LA	language acquisition
Adv	adverb	L1A	first language acquisition
AE	american English	L2A	second language acquisition
Aux	auxiliary	LX	any language
B	bilingualism	LY	any other language
BE	British English	ME	Middle English
c	consonant	M1	first margin of the syllable
CD	colloquial dialect	M2	second margin of the syllable
Co	object complement	n	nucleus of the syllable
Cs	subject complement	N	noun
D	dialect	NP	noun phrase
D1	first dialect	O	object
D2	second dialect	OE	Old English
D3	third dialect	POA	point of articulalation
FL	foreign language	Pr	pronoun
FLA	foreign language acquisition	Prep	preposition
IC	immediate constituent	S	subject
IF	informationally false	SB	sociental bilingualism
Int	interjection	SC	syntactically correct
IT	informationally true	SD	standard dialect
L	language	SW	syntactically wrong
L1	first language	v	vowel
L2	second language	V	verb
L3	third language	VP	verb phrase

APPENDIX II
SYMBOLS

< > A sign to include graphemes or orthographic writing

[ ] A sign to include allophones or phonetic writing

/ / A sign to include phonemes or phonemic writing

{ } A sign to include morphemes

⊃ A sign indicating *implies* or *includes*

= A sign indicating *synonymous with*

⇔ A sign indicating *antonymous with*

∴ A sign indicating *therefore*

* A sign indicating non-grammaticality

APPENDIX III
ENGLISH PHONEMES

1.	/p/	pen	21.	/ ŋ /	sing
2.	/ b/	ban	22.	/w/	window
3.	/t/	ten	23.	/r/	right
4.	/d/	down	24.	/y/	/yet/
5.	/k/	kite	25.	/i/	bit
6.	/g/	good	26.	/ e/	bet
7.	/č/	chair	27.	/ æ/	hat
8.	/ ǰ/	judge	28.	/ ɨ /	wanted
9.	/ ɵ/	thin	29.	/ ə /	the
10.	/ ð /	the	30.	/ a/	far
11.	/f/	fine	31.	/ u /	put
12.	/v/	very	32.	/ ow/	boat
13.	/h/	hat	33.	/ ɔw/	bought
14.	/s/	sign	34.	/iy/	seat
15.	/z/	zoo	35.	/ey/	same
16.	/š /	shine	36.	/ay/	fine
17.	/ž /	treasure	37.	/uw/	pool
18.	/l/	late	38.	/ aw/	found
19.	/ m/	mine	39.	/ oy/	soil
20.	/ n/	now			

APPENDIX IV
ARABIC PHONEMES

1. / t / ت
2. / T / ط
3. /k / ك
4. / q/ ق
5. / ? / ء
6. / b / ب
7. / d / د
8. / D / ض
9. /ǰ/ ج
10. / f / ف
11. / Ɵ / ث
12. /s / س
13. / S / ص
14. / š / ش
15. / x / خ
16. / H / ح
17. /h/ ه

18. / ð / ذ
19. / z/ ز
20. /Đ/ ظ
21. /G/ غ
22. /9/ ع
23. /m/ م
24. /n/ ن
25. /l/ ل
26. /r/ ر
27. /w/ و (ولد)
28. /y/ ي (يد)
29. /i/ □
30. /a/ □
31. /u/ □
32. /i:/ ي (سليم)
33. /a:/ ا (سار)
34. /u:/ و (يدنو)

Subject Index

The Author's Books

1. *The Light of Islam*

2. *The Need for Islam*

3. *Traditions of Prophet Muhammad /B1*

4. *Traditions of Prophet Muhammad /B2*
5. *The Truth about Jesus Christ*

6. *Islam and Christianity*

7. *A Dictionary of Islamic Terms: English-Arabic & Arabic-English*

8. *A Dictionary of the Holy Quran: Arabic-English*
9. *Questions and answers about Islam*

10. *Learn Arabic by Yourself*

11. *Simplified English Grammar*

12. *A Dictionary of Education: English- Arabic*

13. *A Dictionary of Theoretical Linguistics: English- Arabic*

14. *A Dictionary of Applied Linguistics: English-Arabic*

15. *Teaching English to Arab Students*

16. *A Workbook for English Teaching Practice*

17. *Programmed TEFL Methodology*
18. *The Teacher of English*

19. *Improve Your English*

20. *A Workbook for English II*

21. *Advance Your English*

22. *The Blessing of Islam*

23. *An Introduction to Linguistics*

24. *Comparative Linguistics: English and Arabic*
25. *A Contrastive Transformational Grammar: English-Arabic*

26. *Why have they chosen Islam?*

53. *English Grammar: Morphology*
54. *General Translation 2: From Arabic into English.*

تطلب جميع كتب الدكتور محمد علي الخولي من دار الفلاح
ص. ب ٨١٨ – صويلح ١١٩١٠- الأردن هاتف وفاكس ٥٤١١٥٤٧-٠٠٩٦٢٦

للاطلاع على هذه الكتب، يمكن زيارة الموقع الالكتروني لدار الفلاح:
www.daralfalah.com

Printed in the United States
By Bookmasters